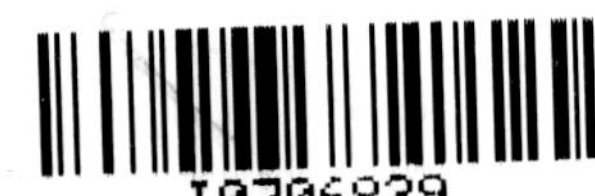

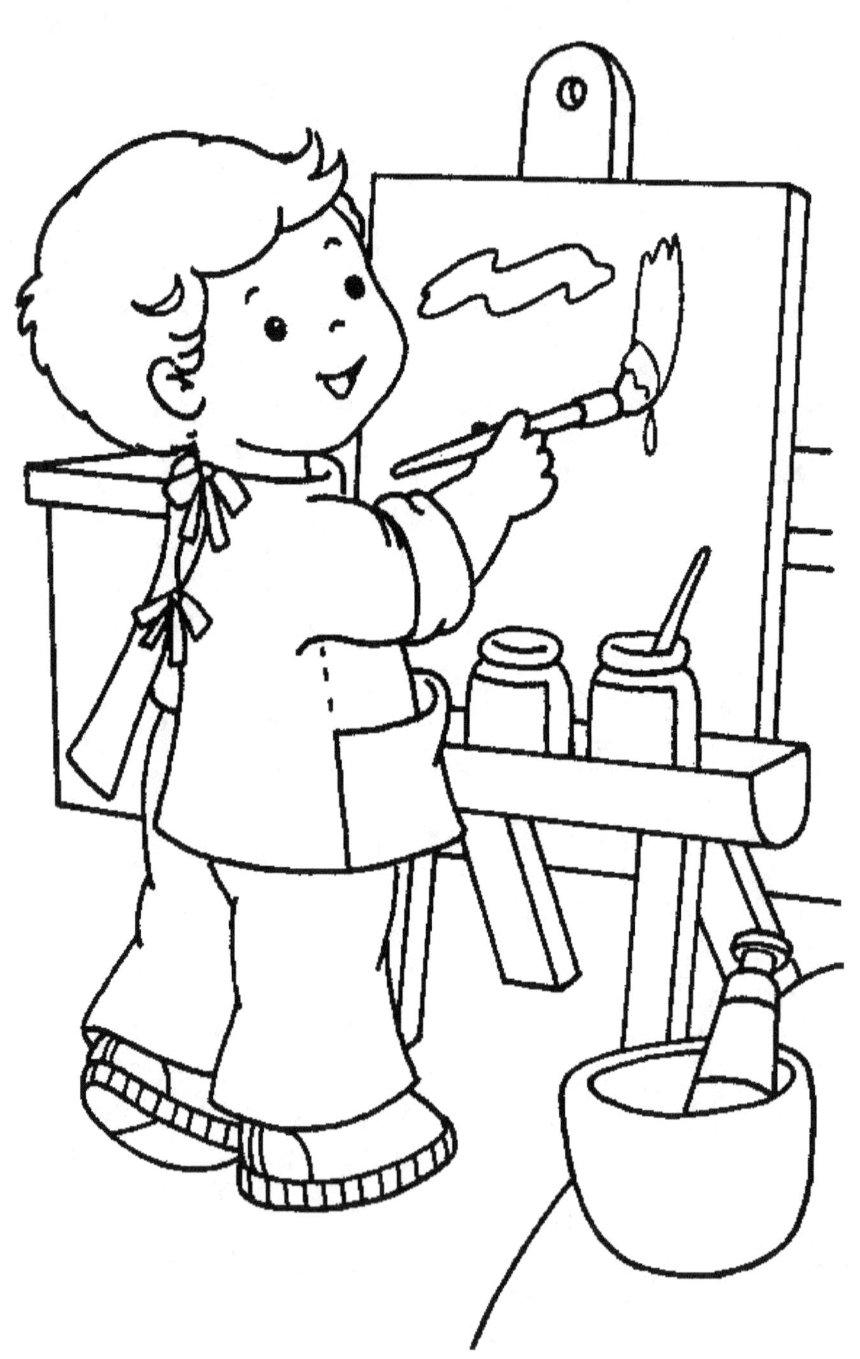

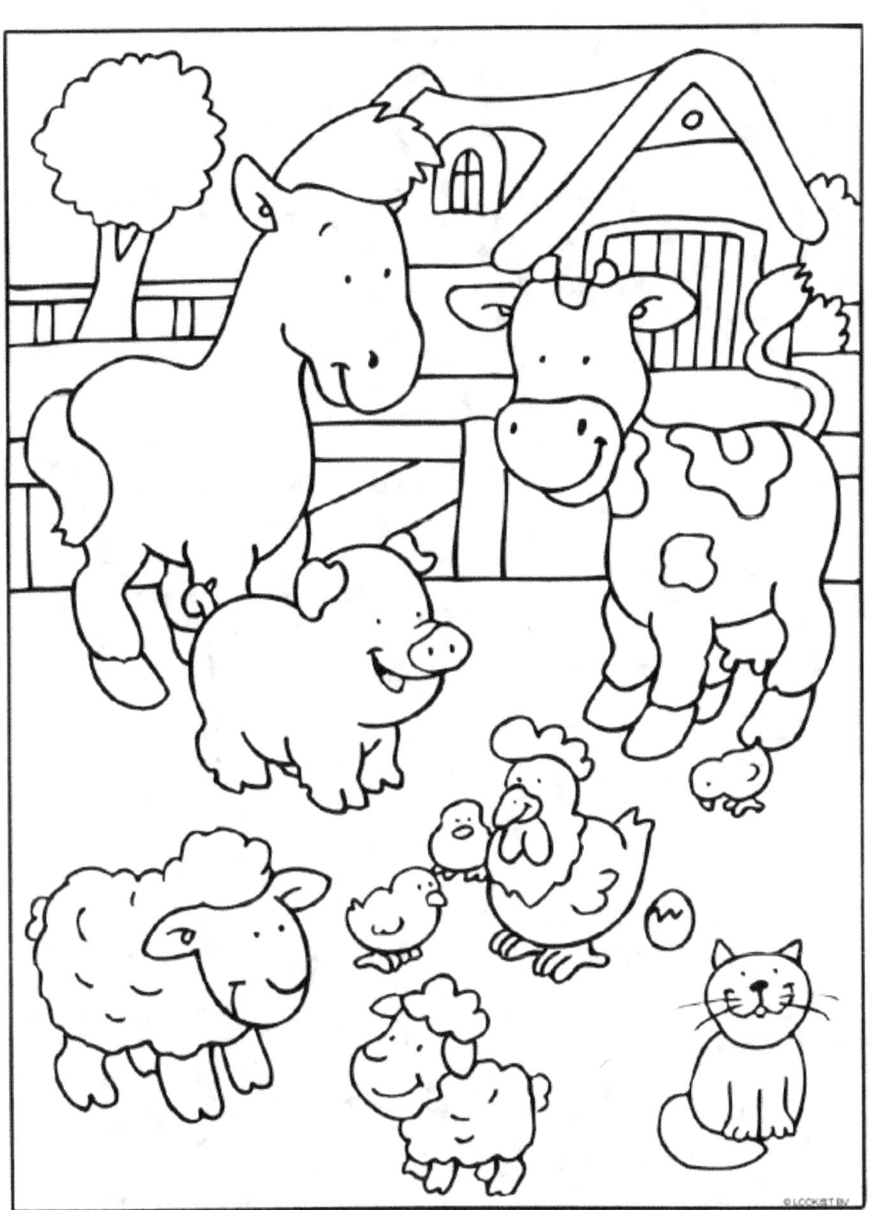

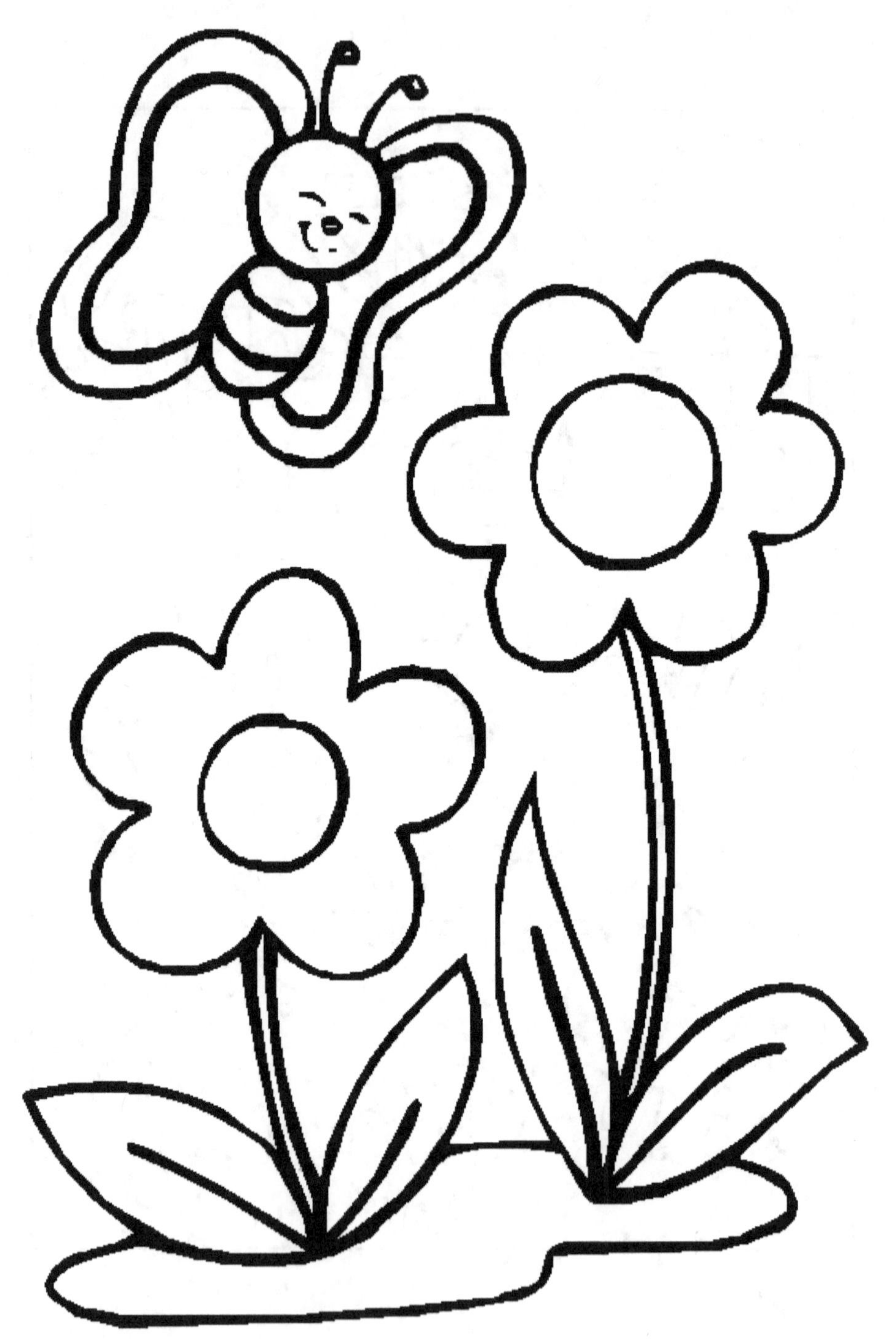

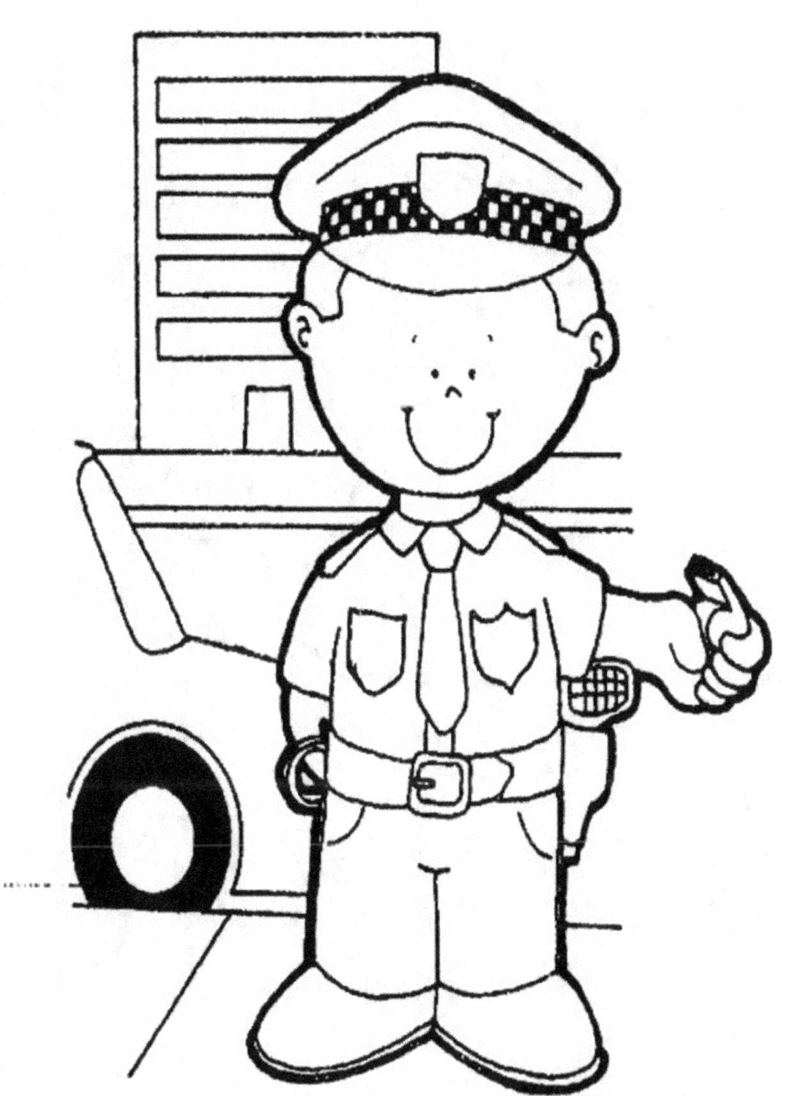

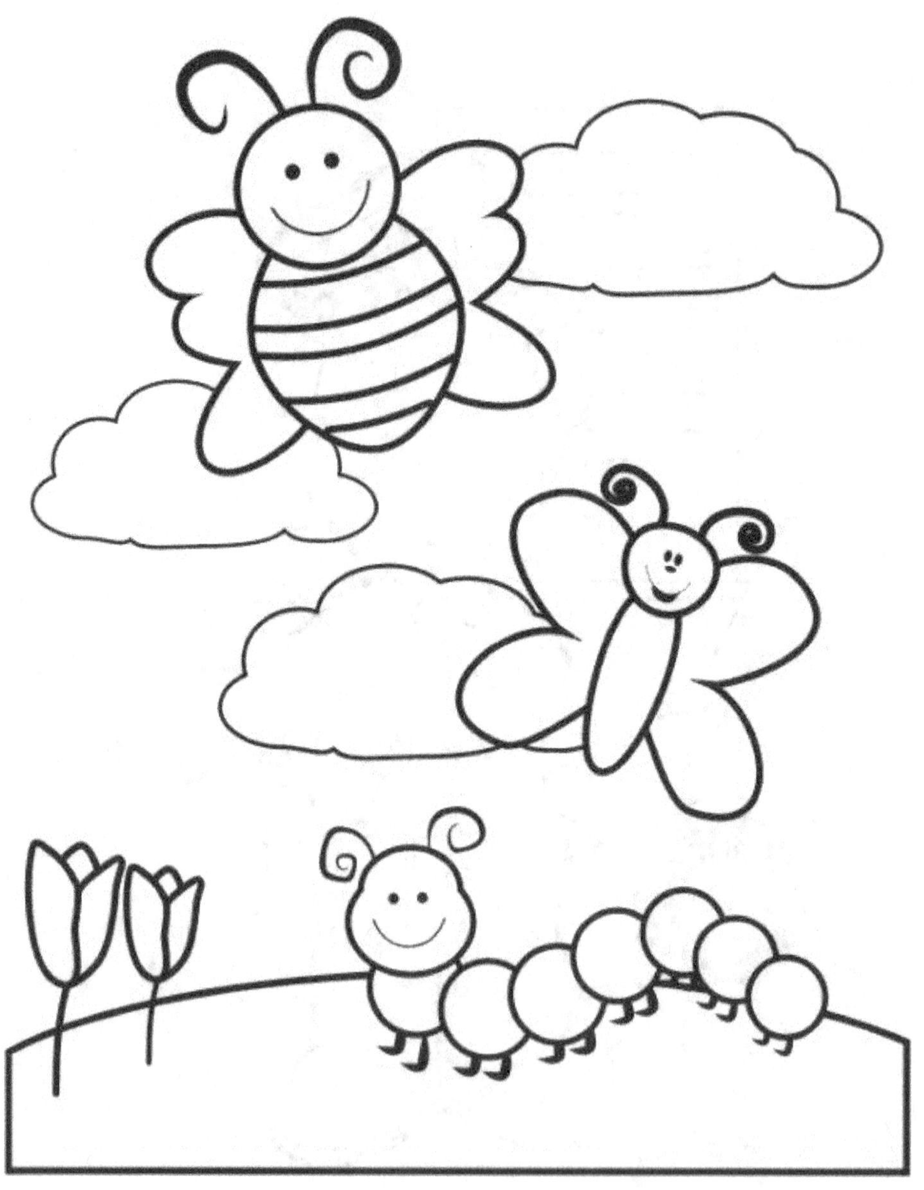

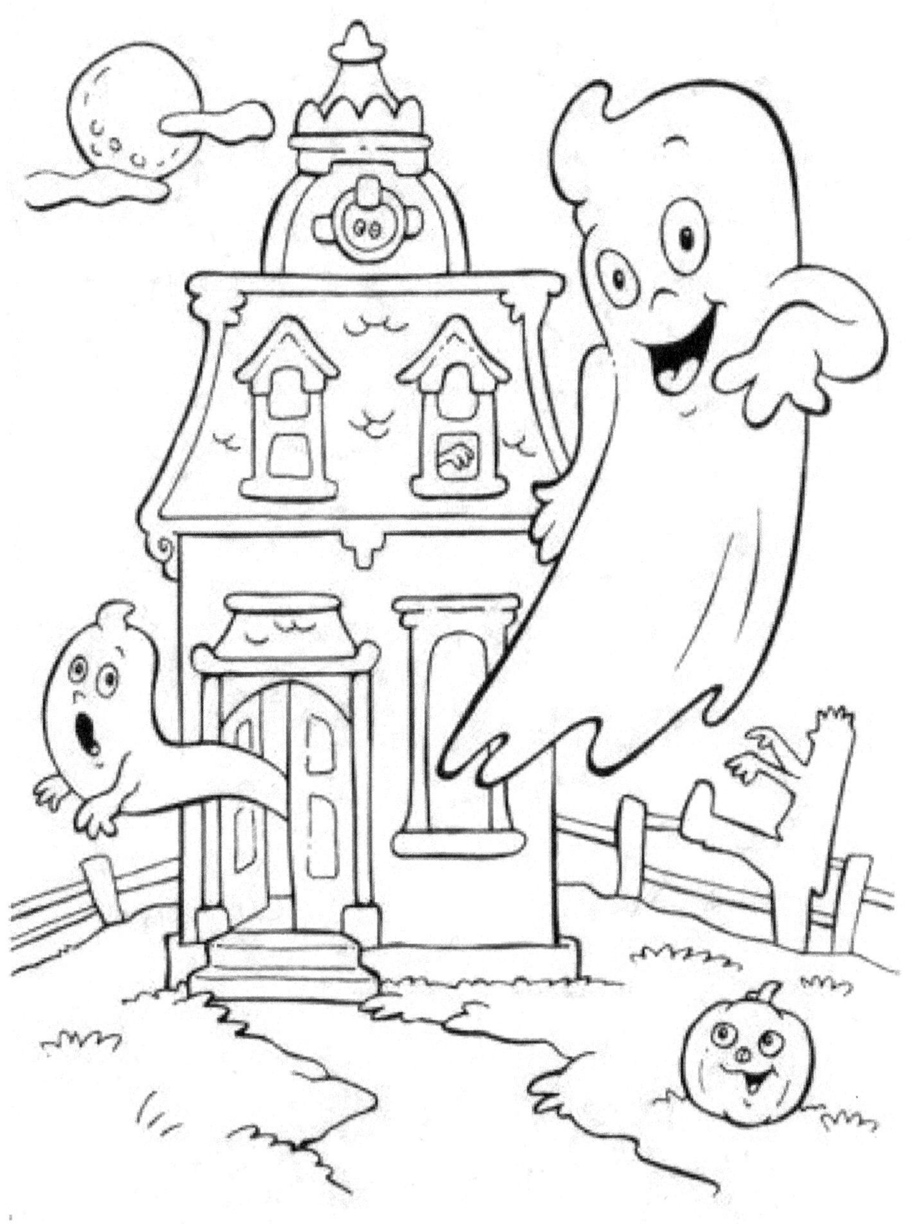

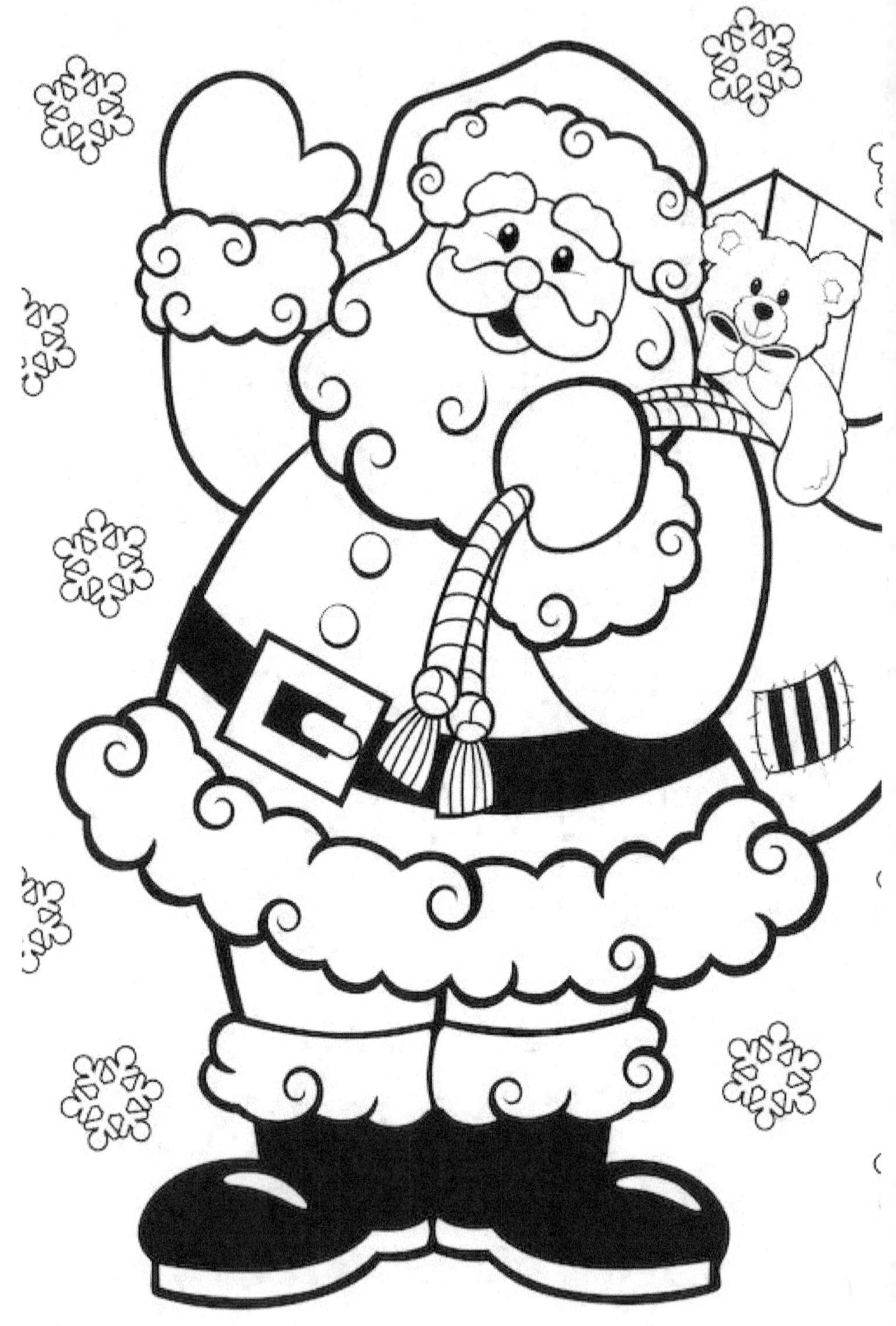

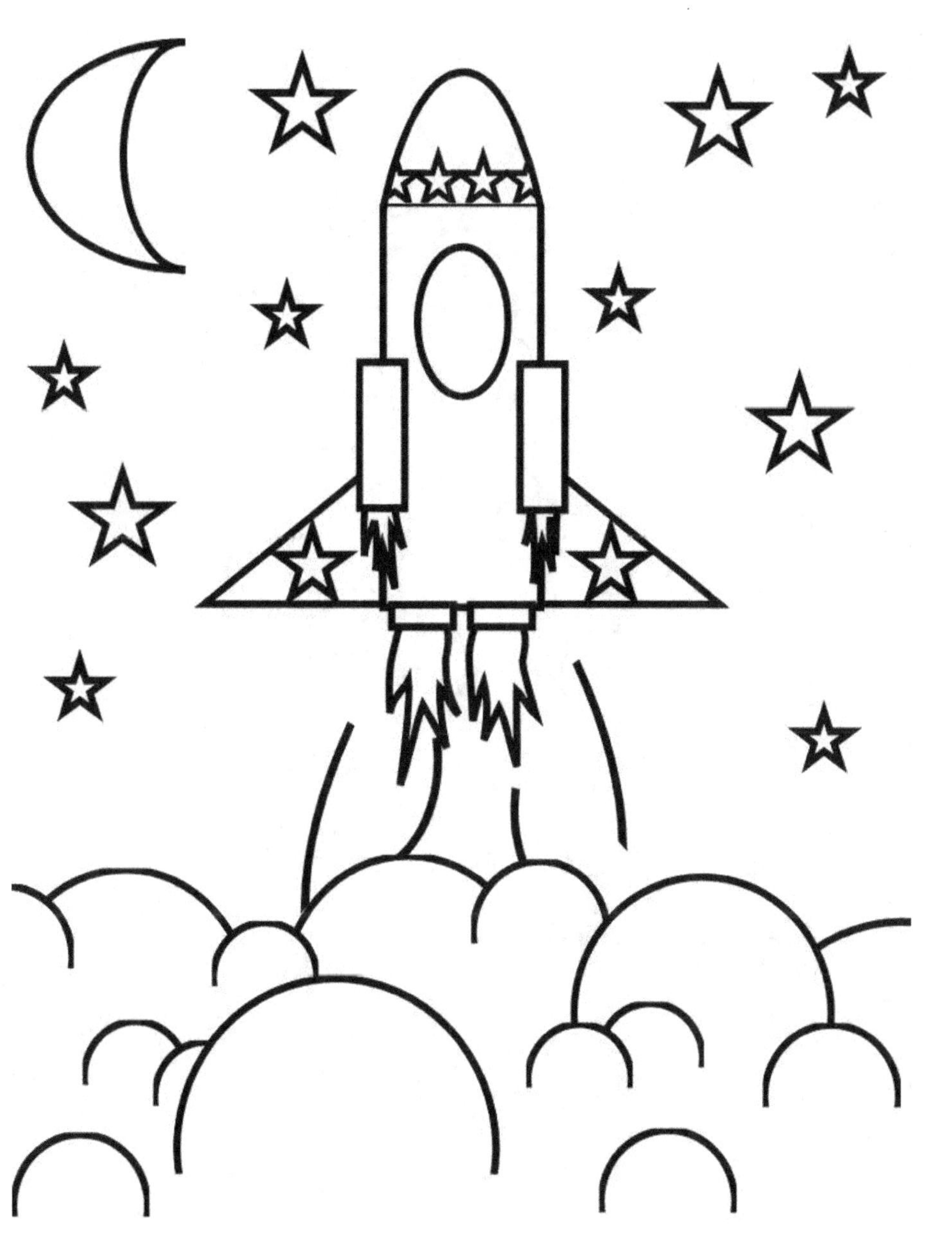

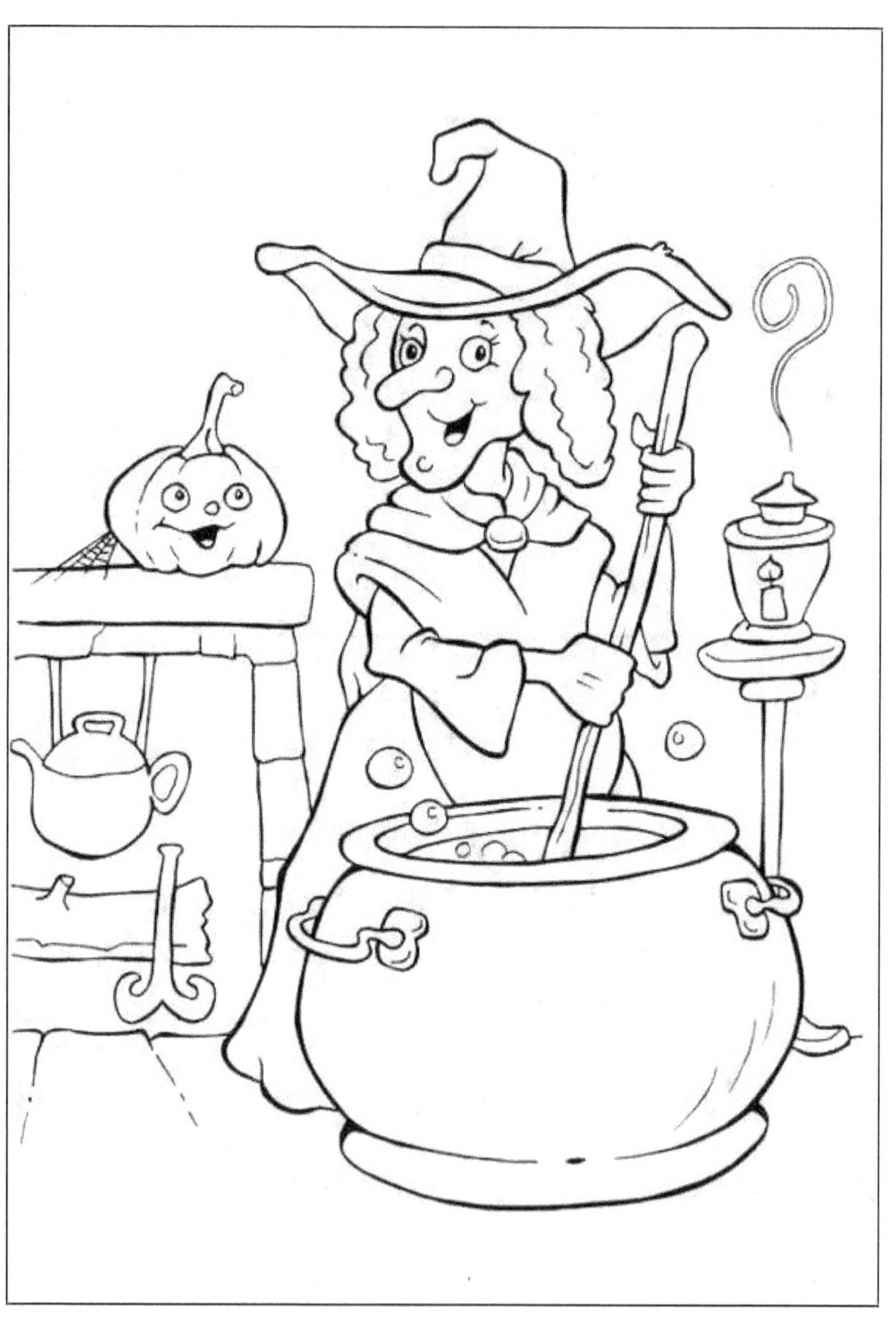

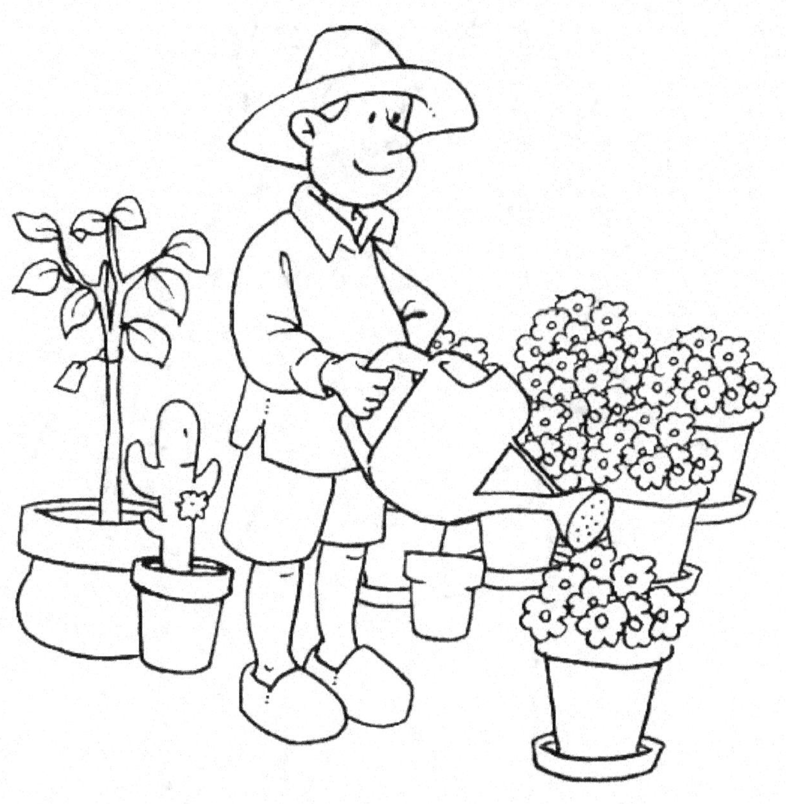

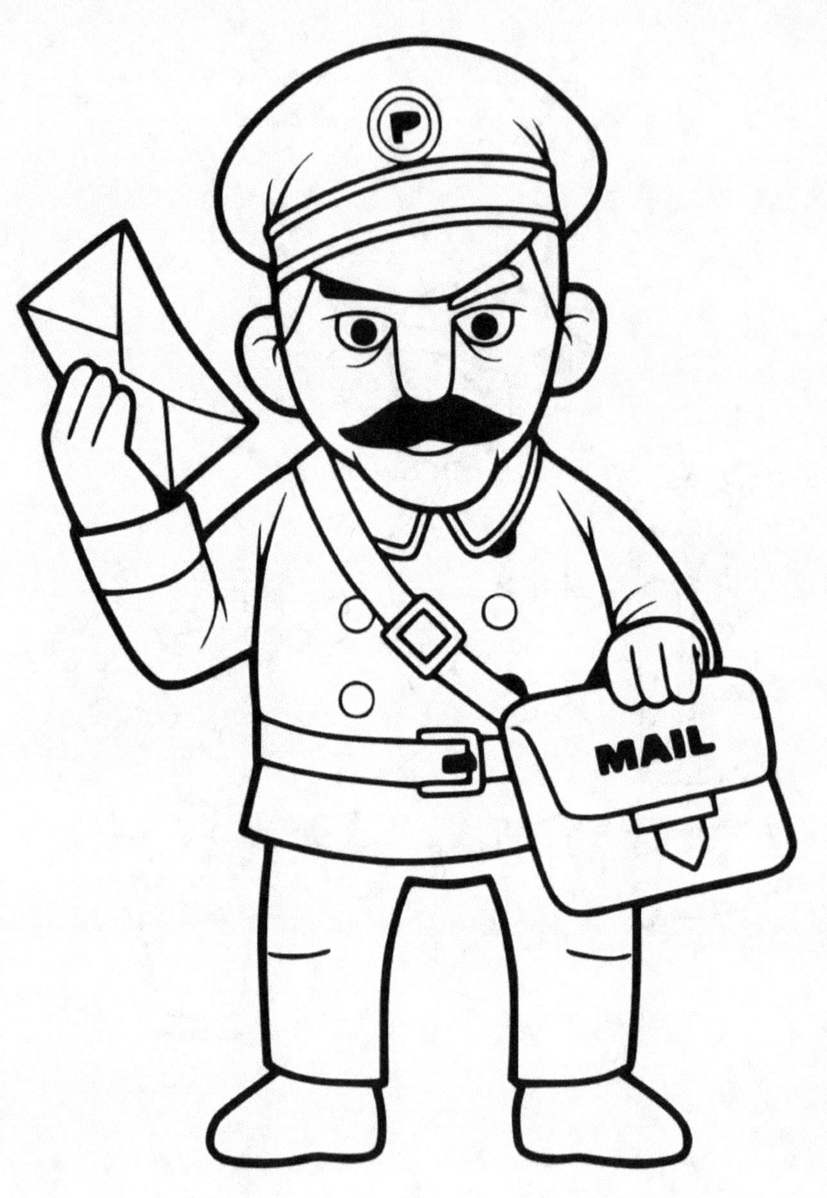

MAIL

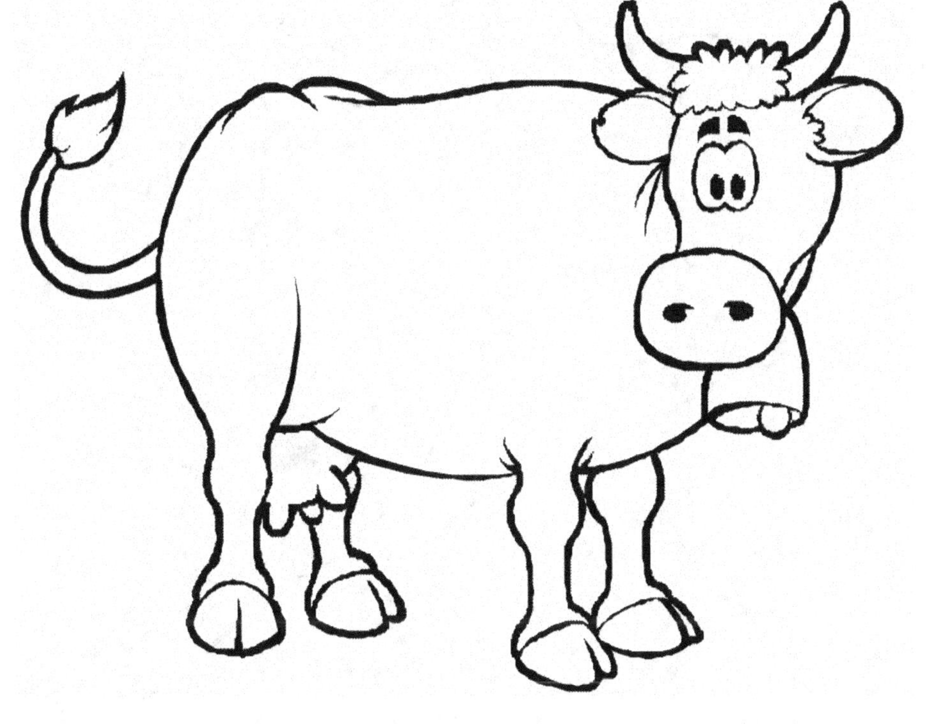

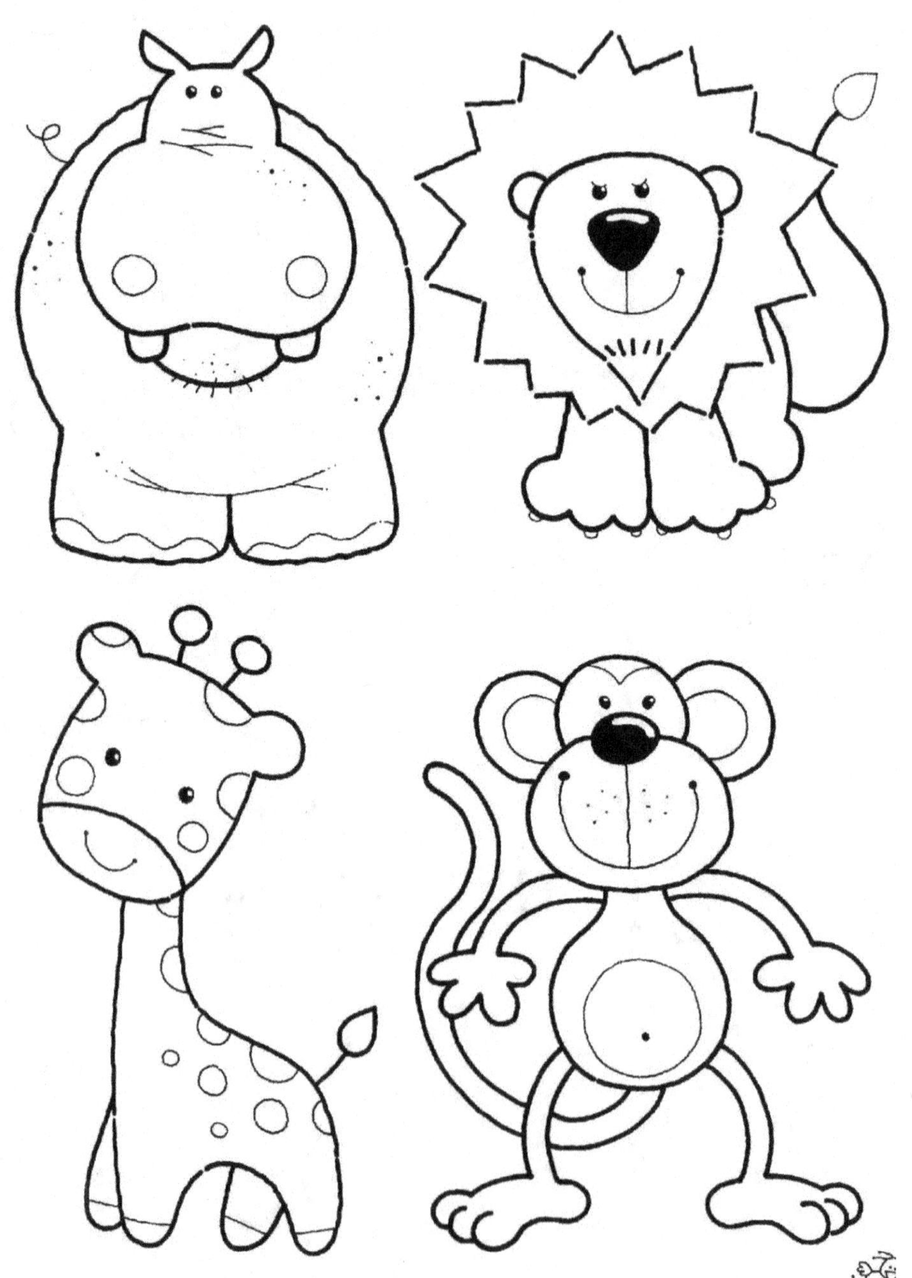

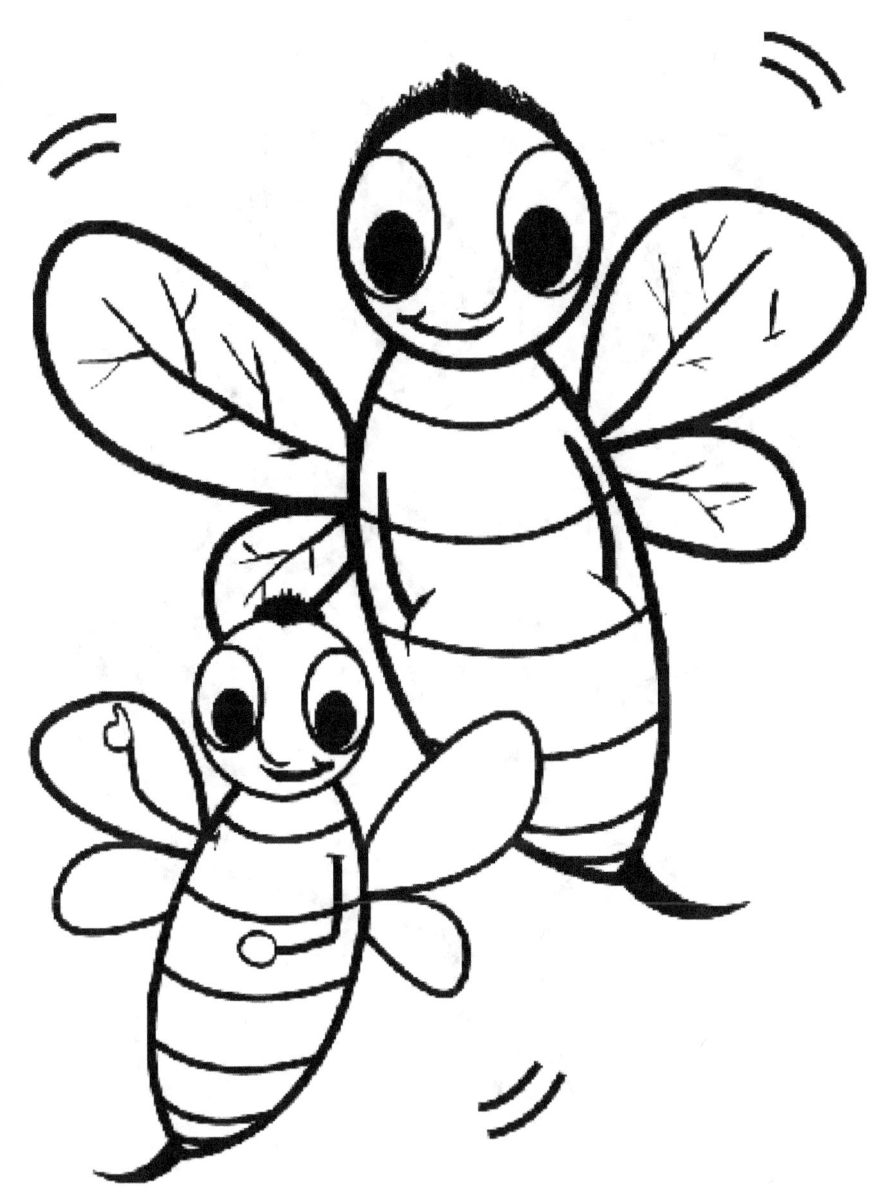

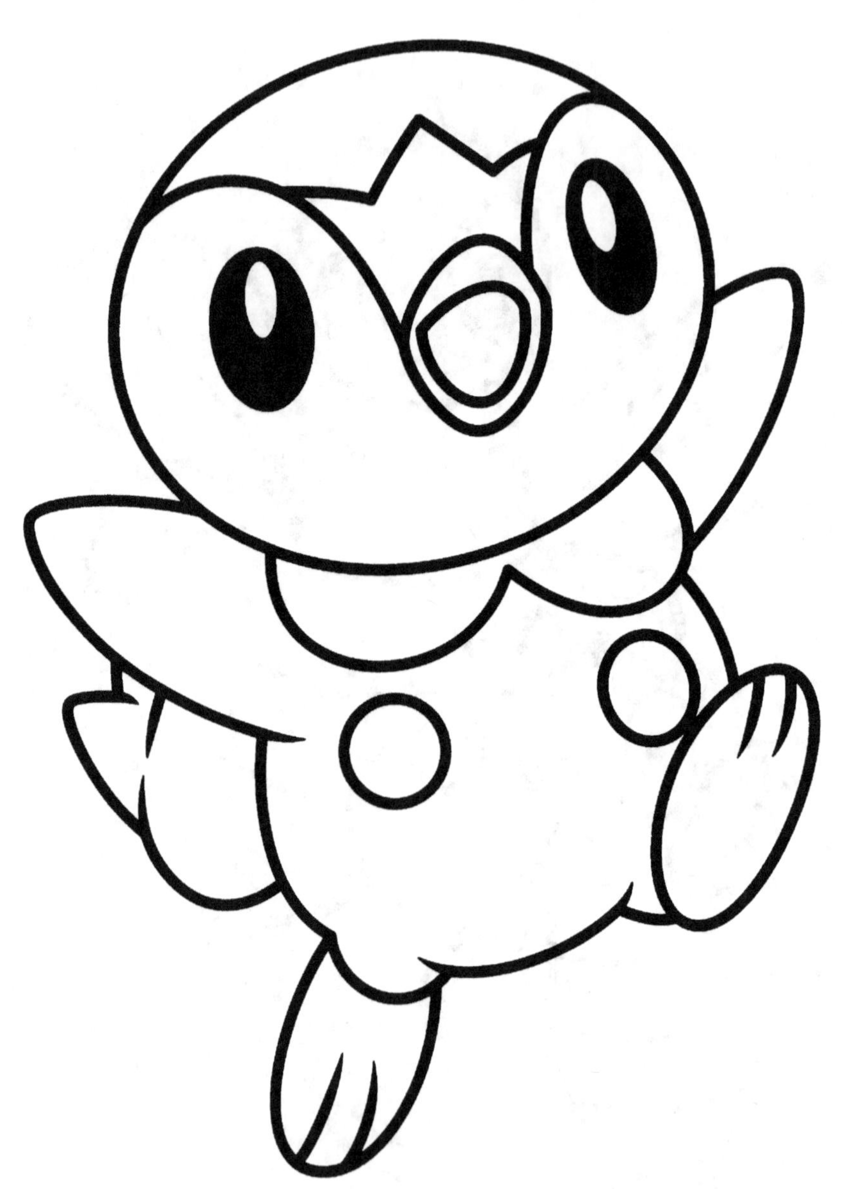

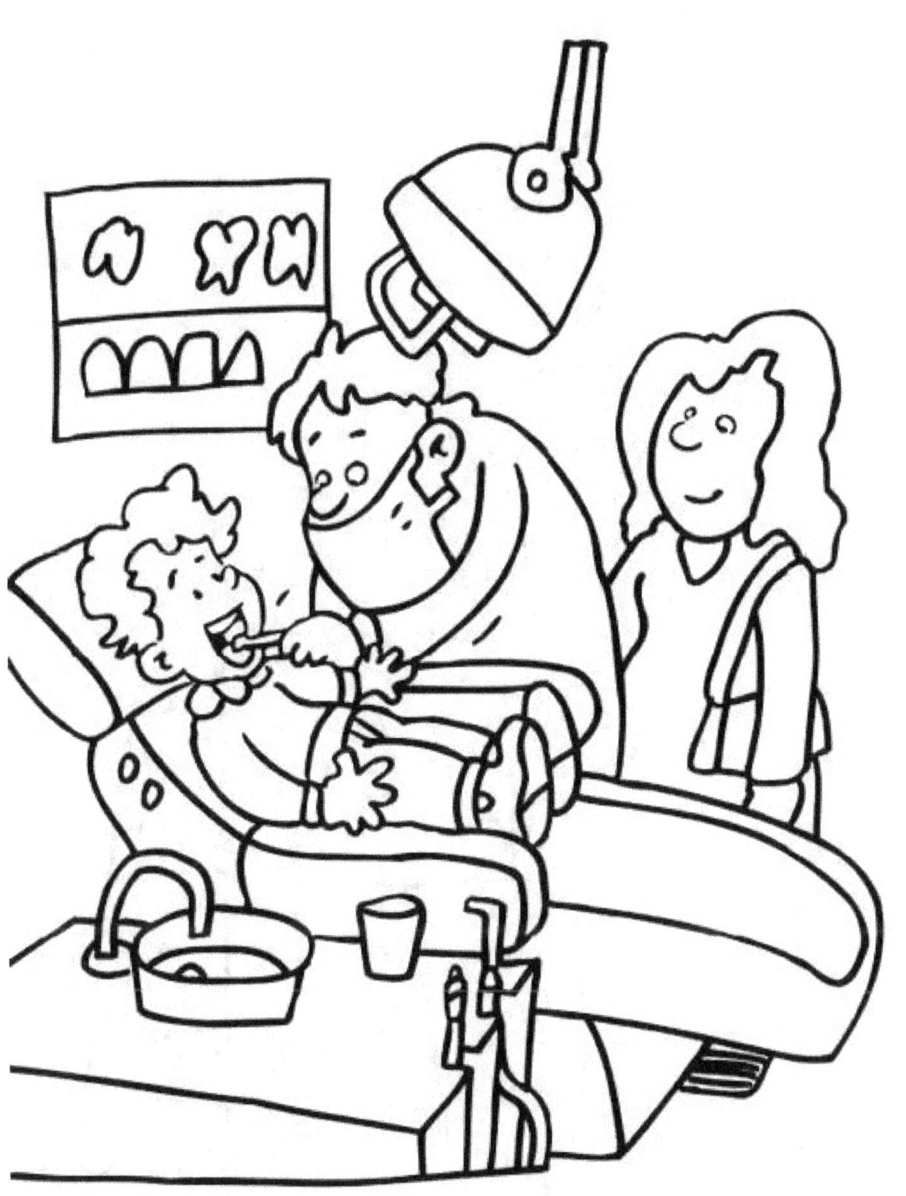

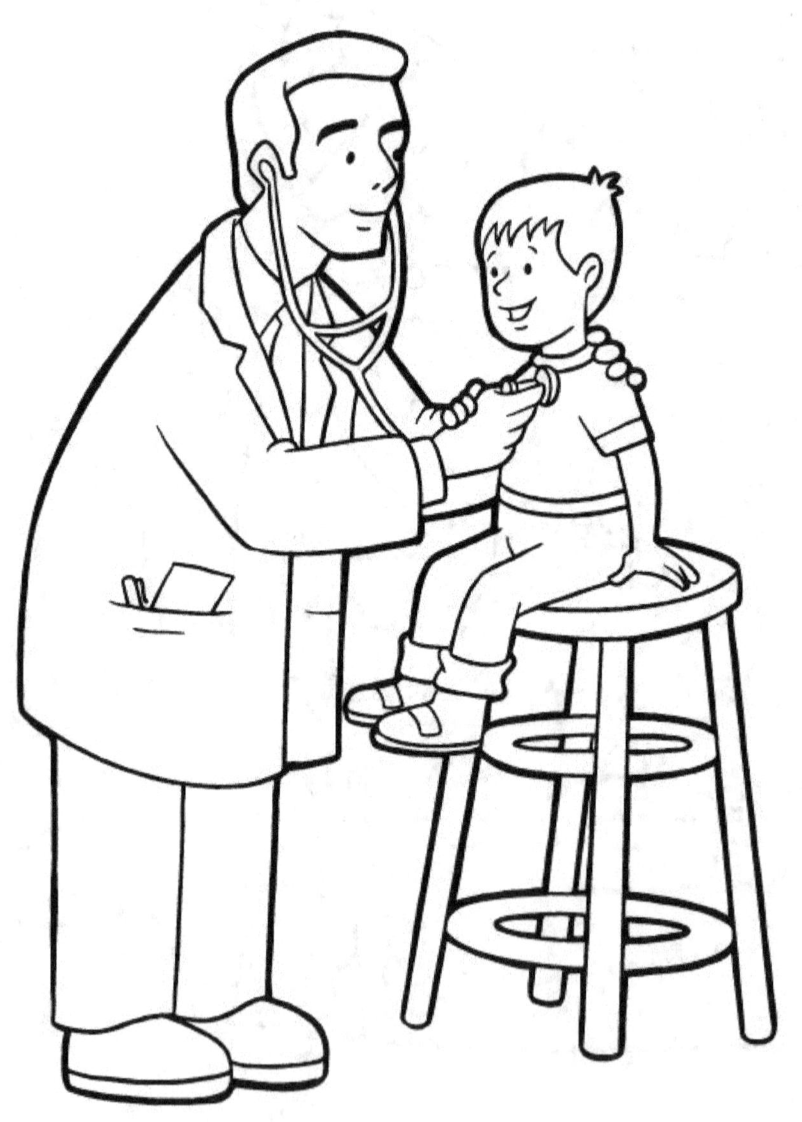

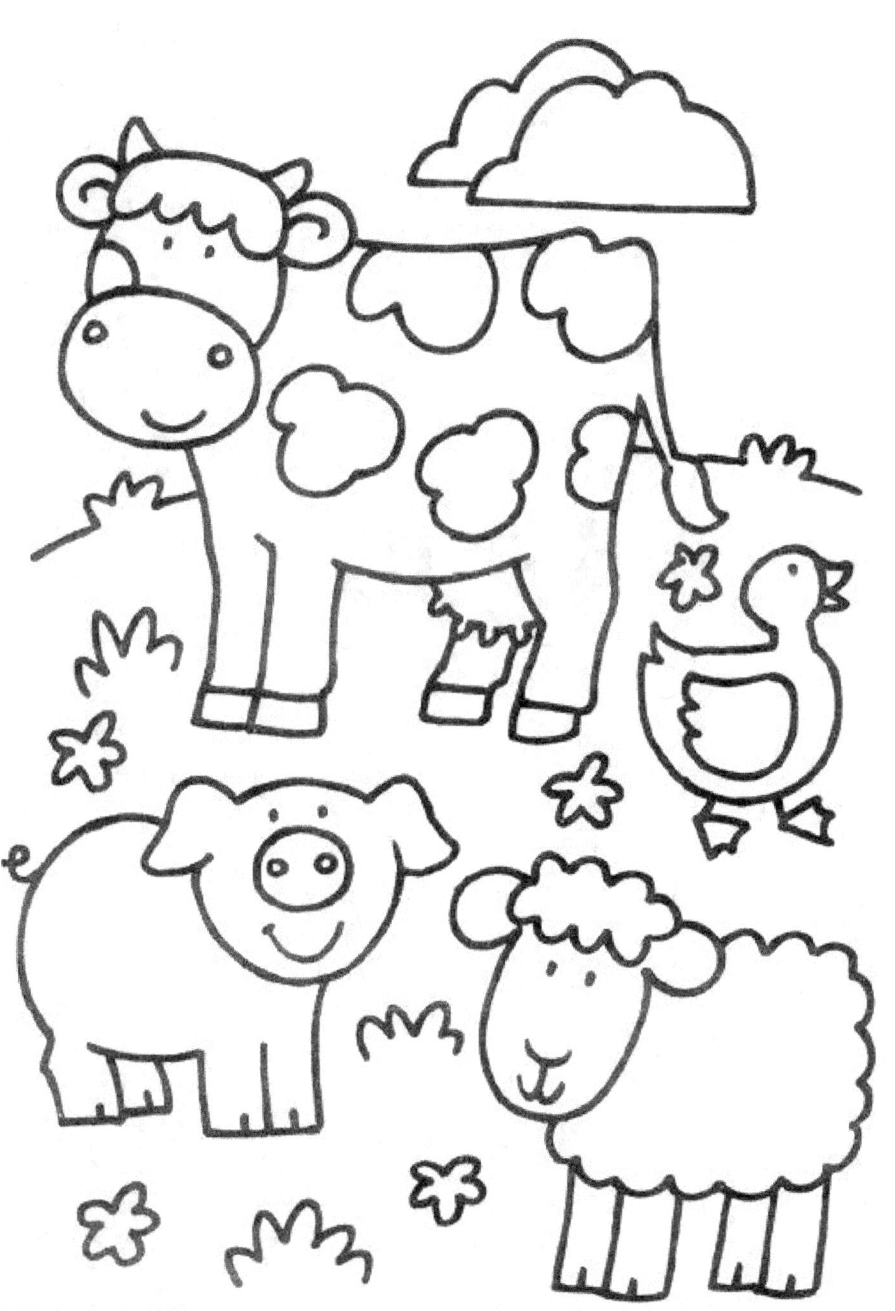

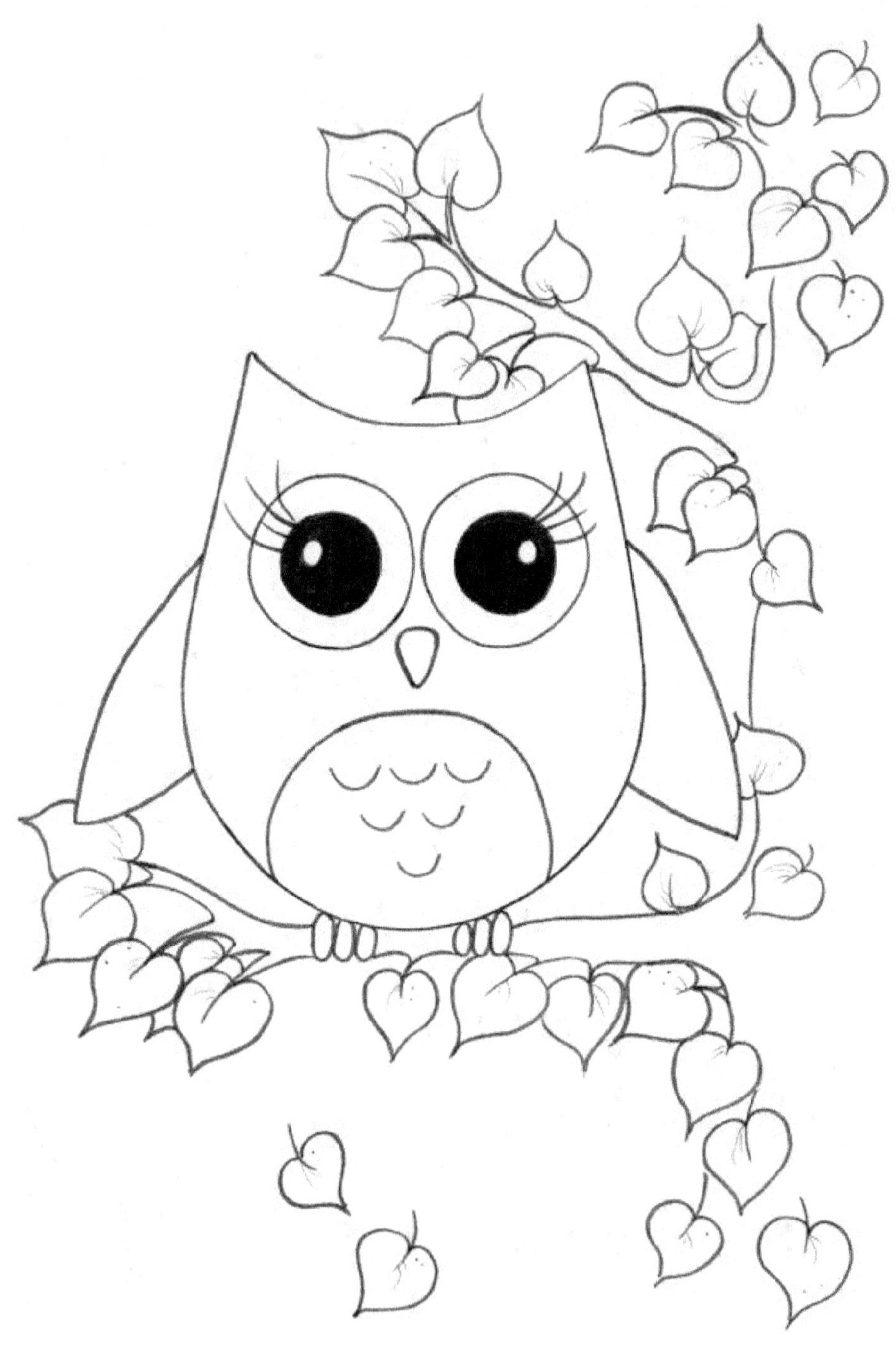

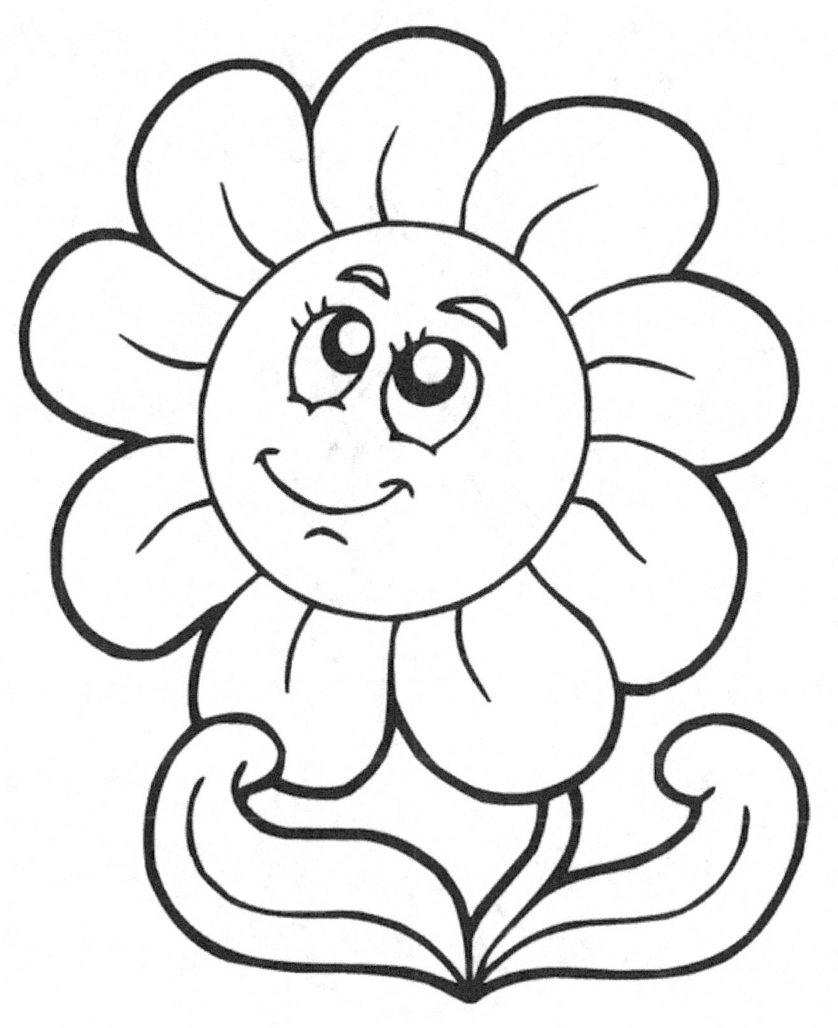

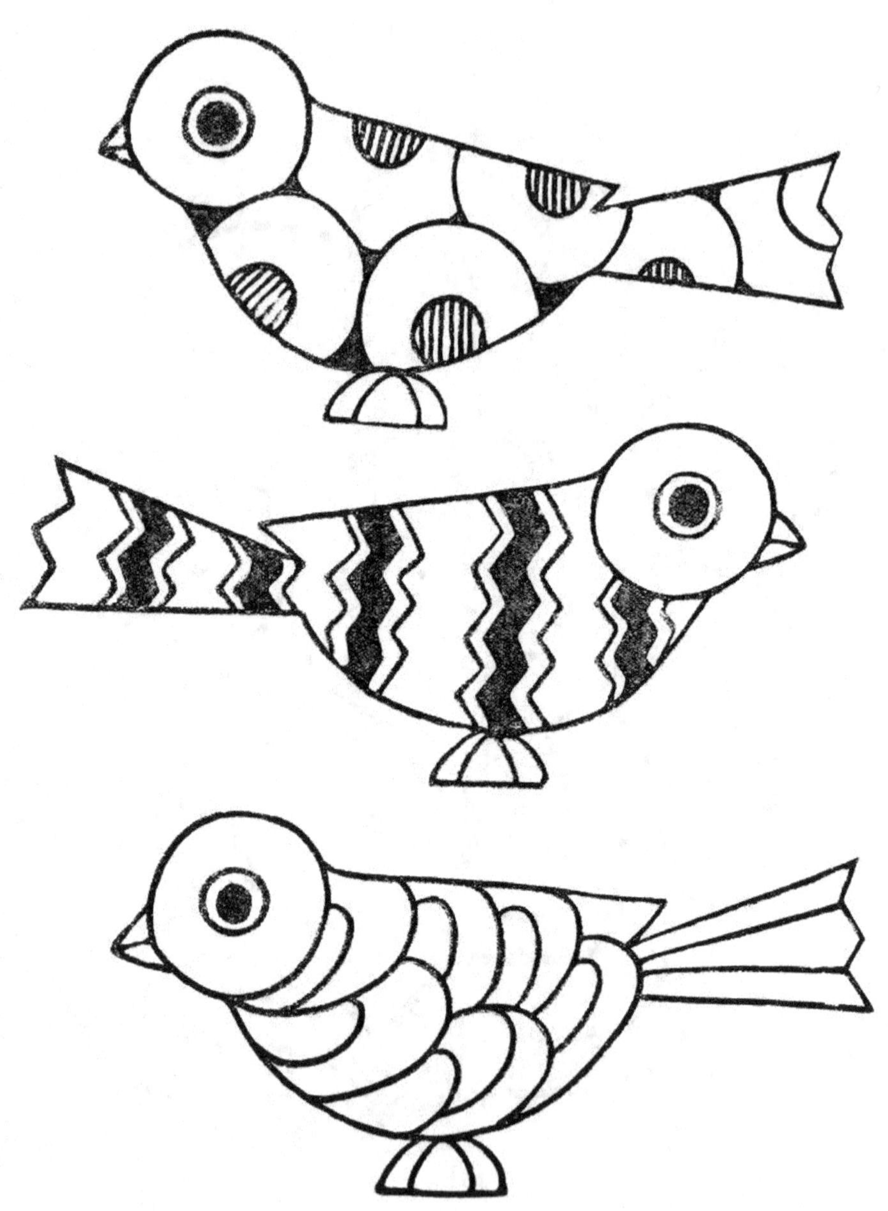

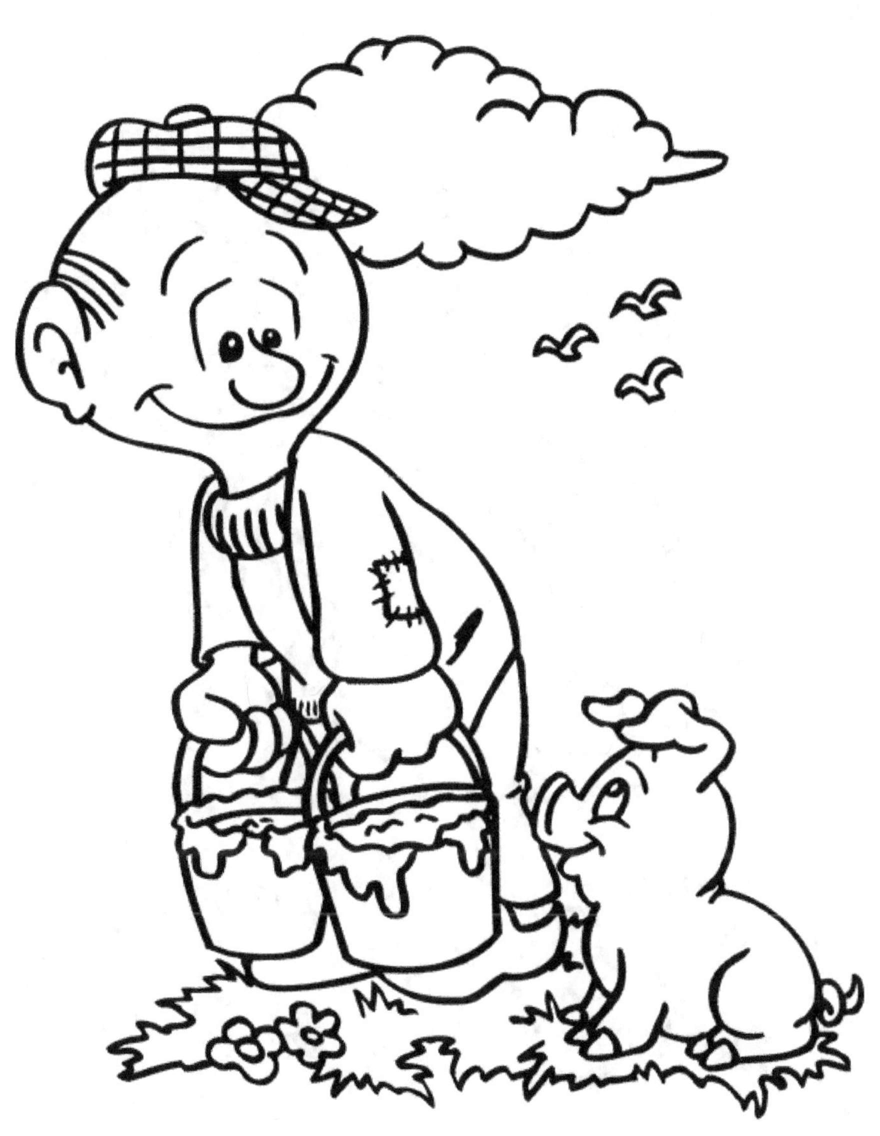

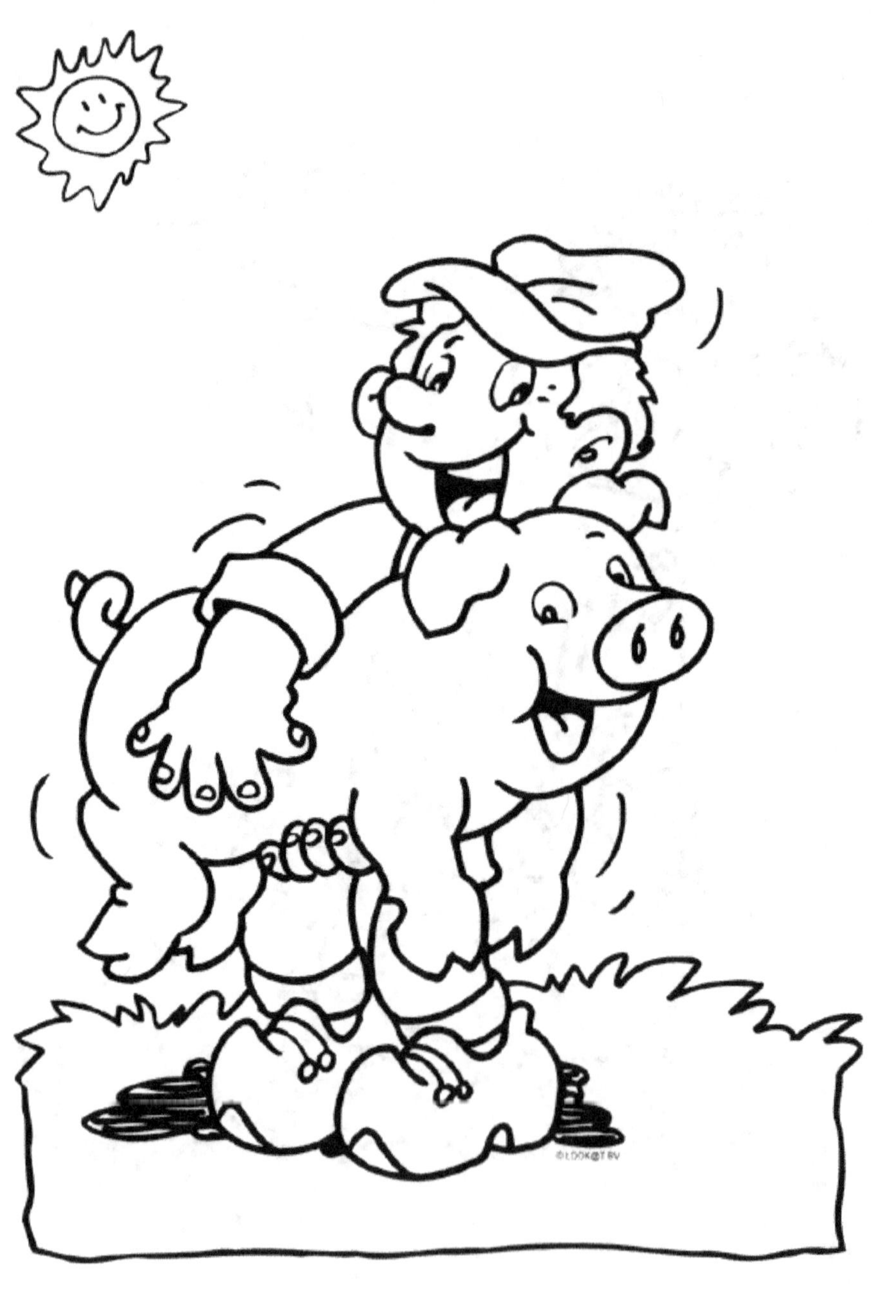

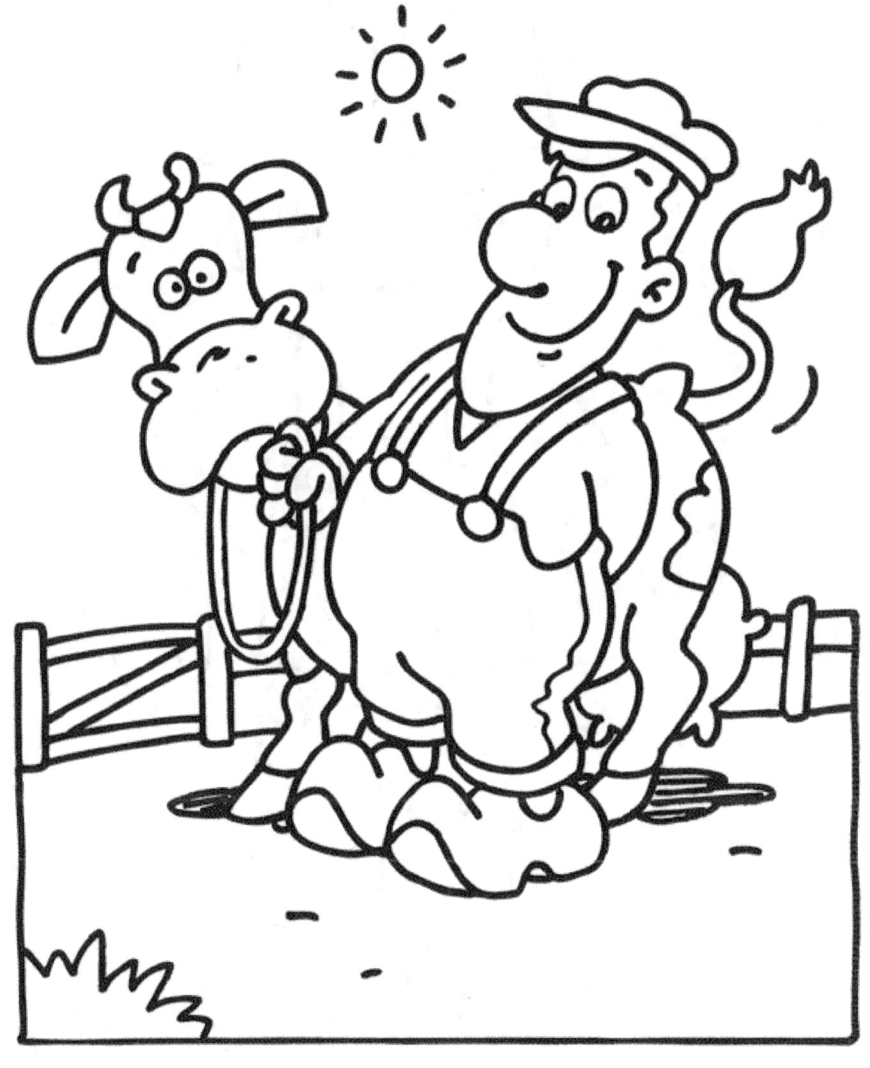

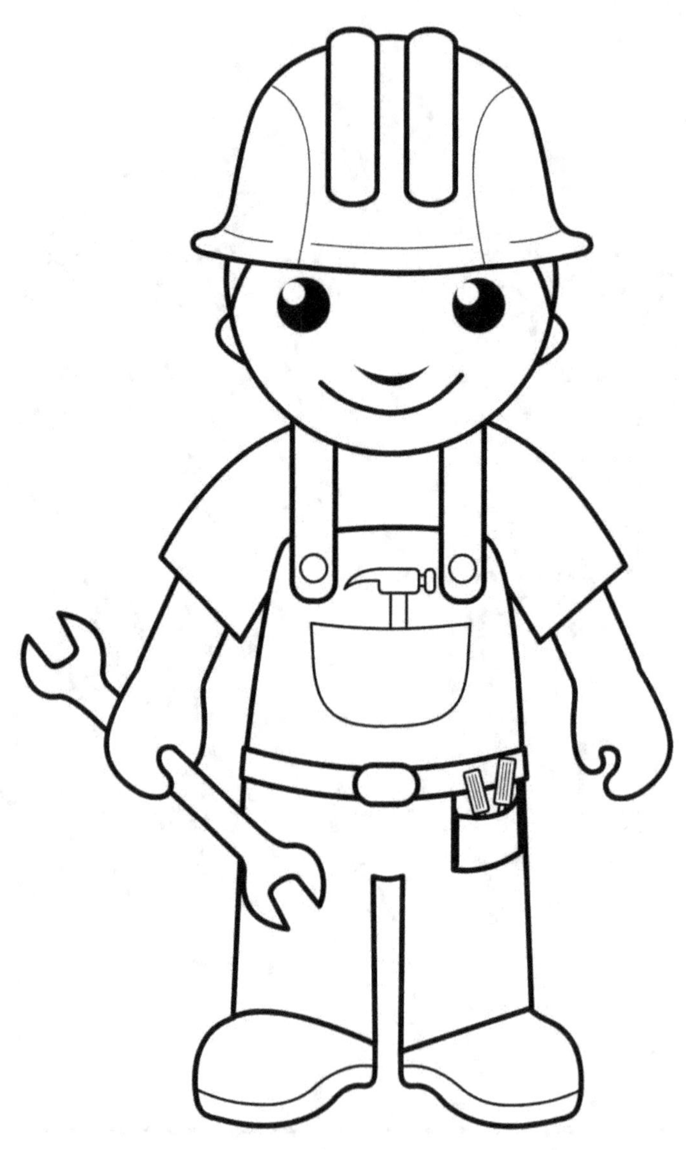

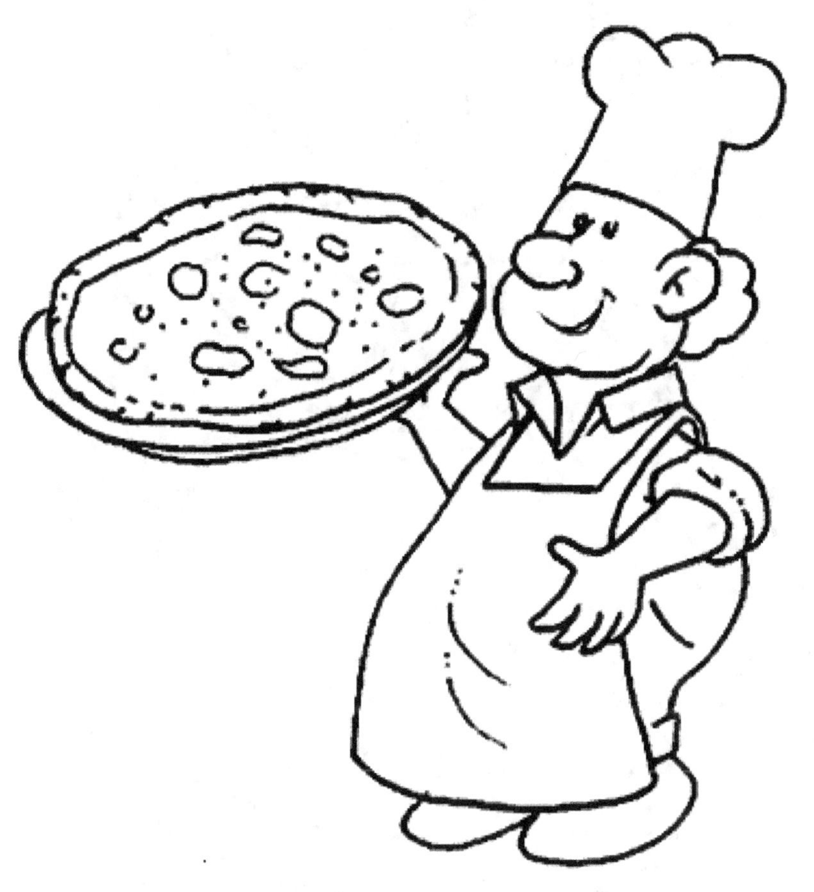

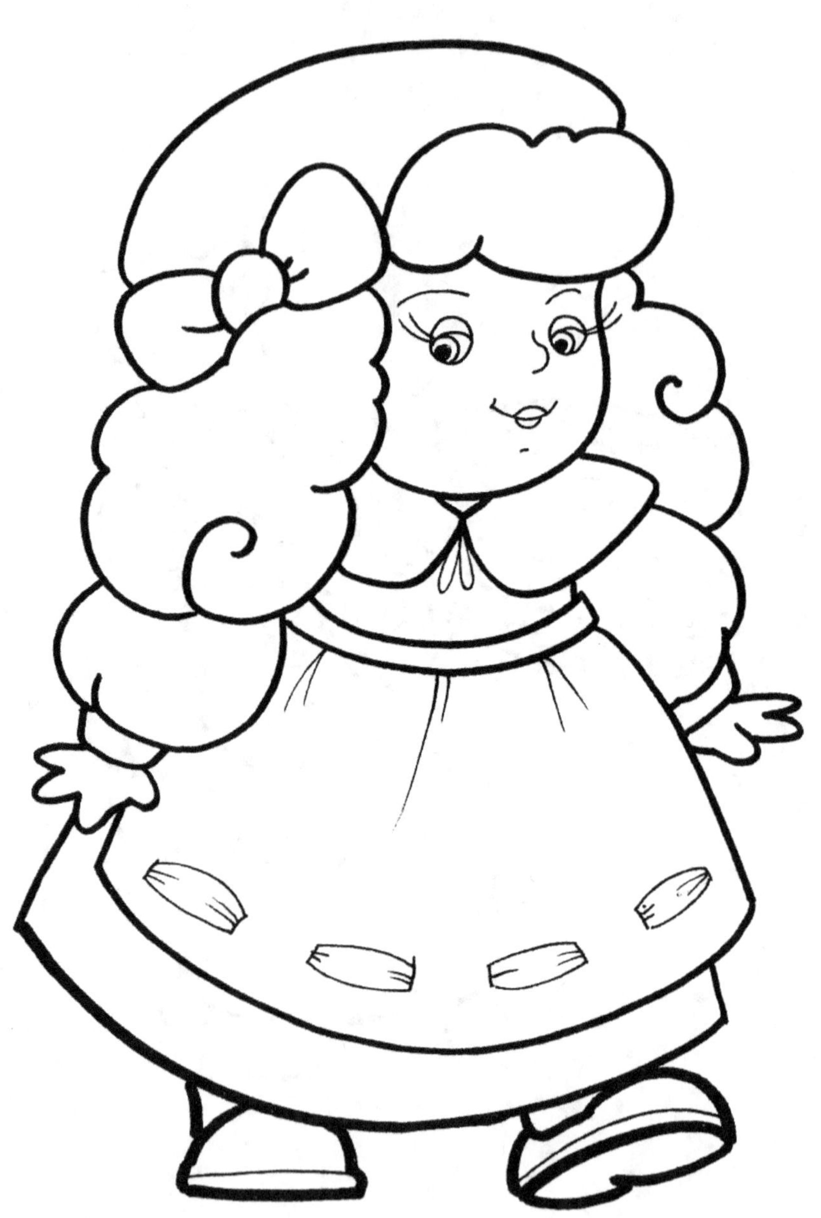

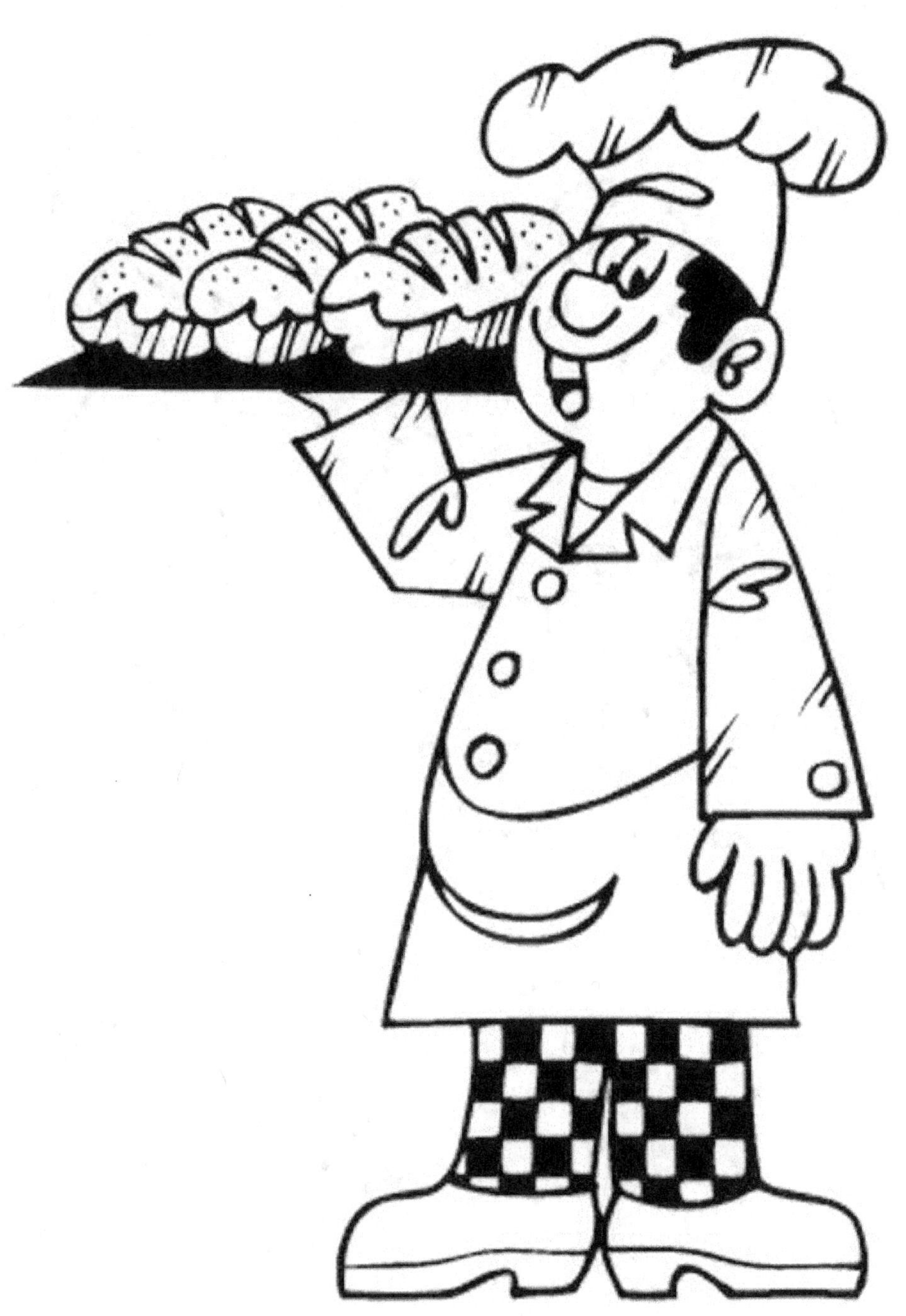

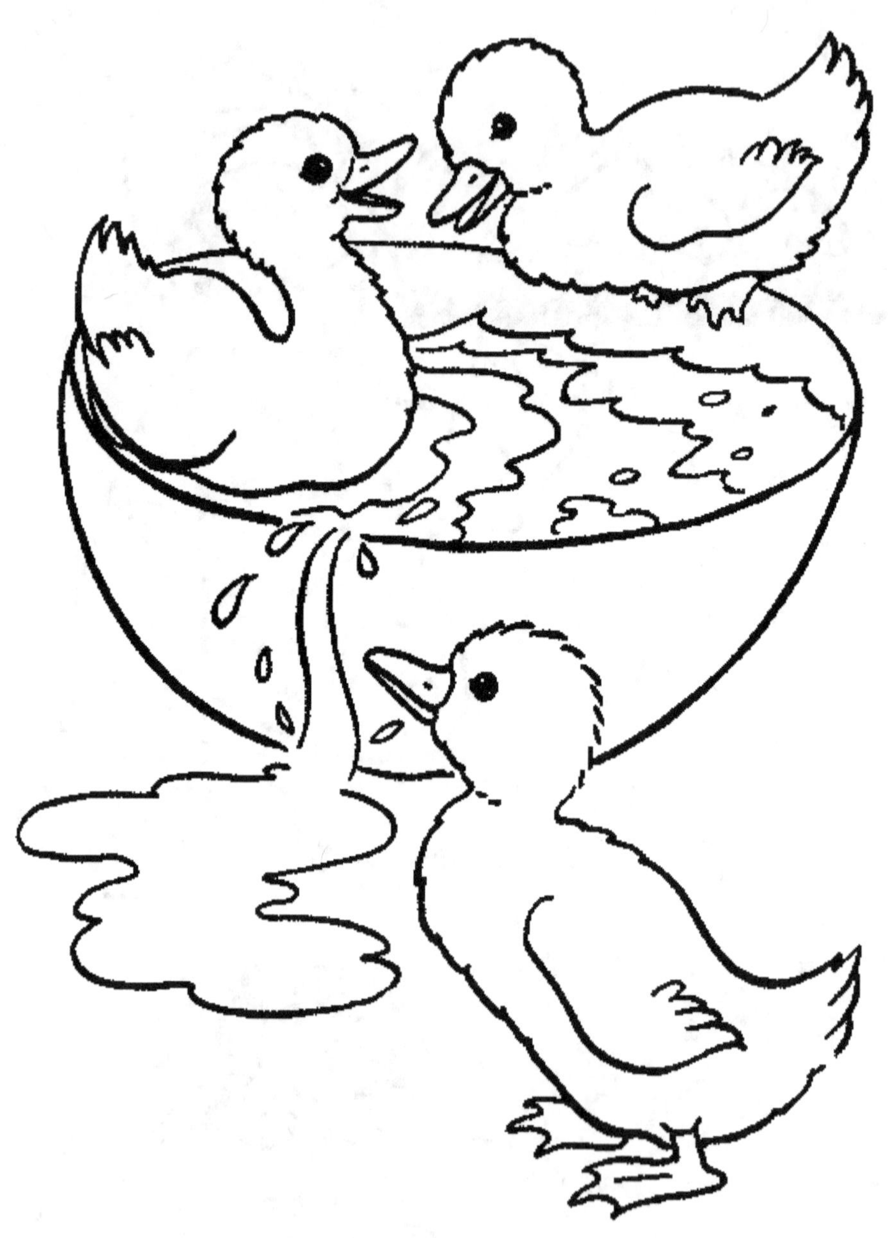

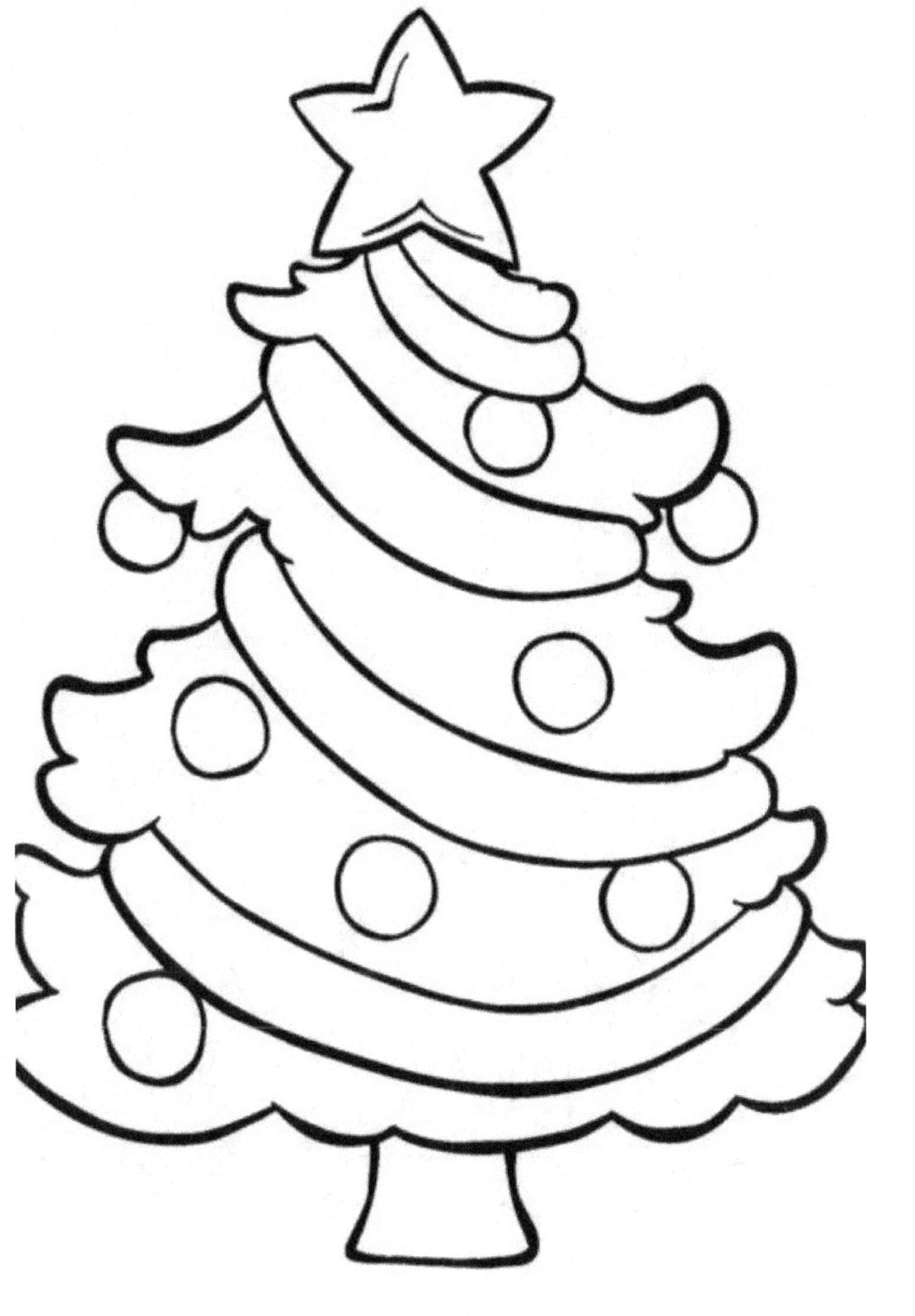

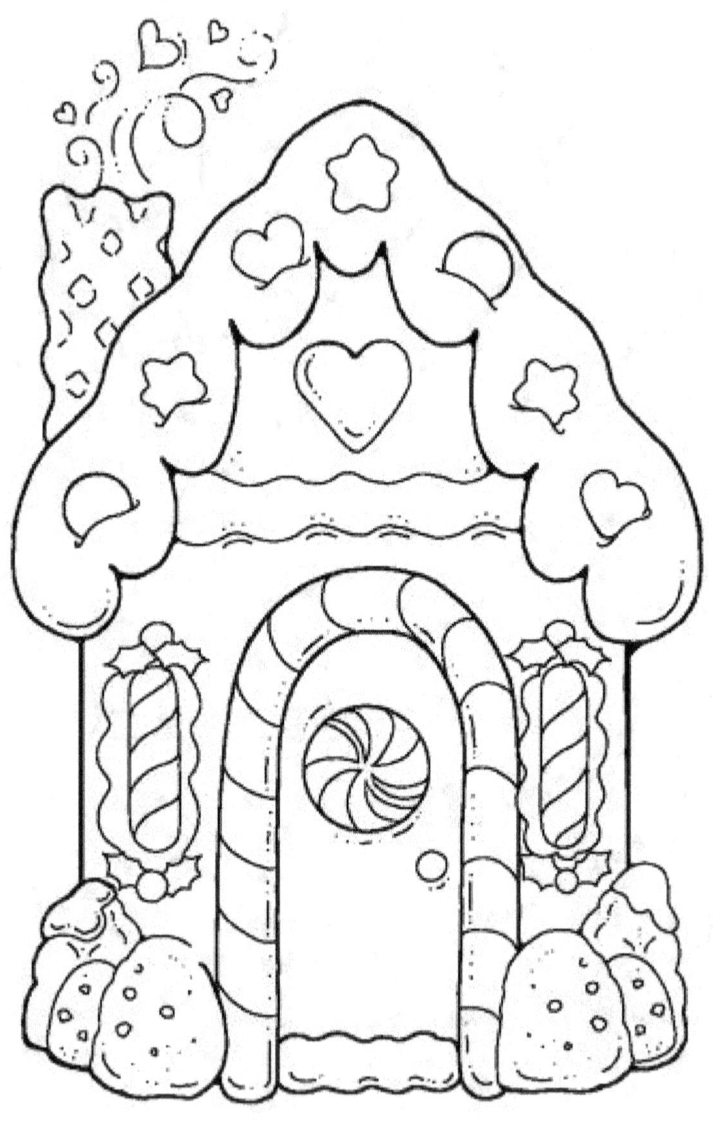

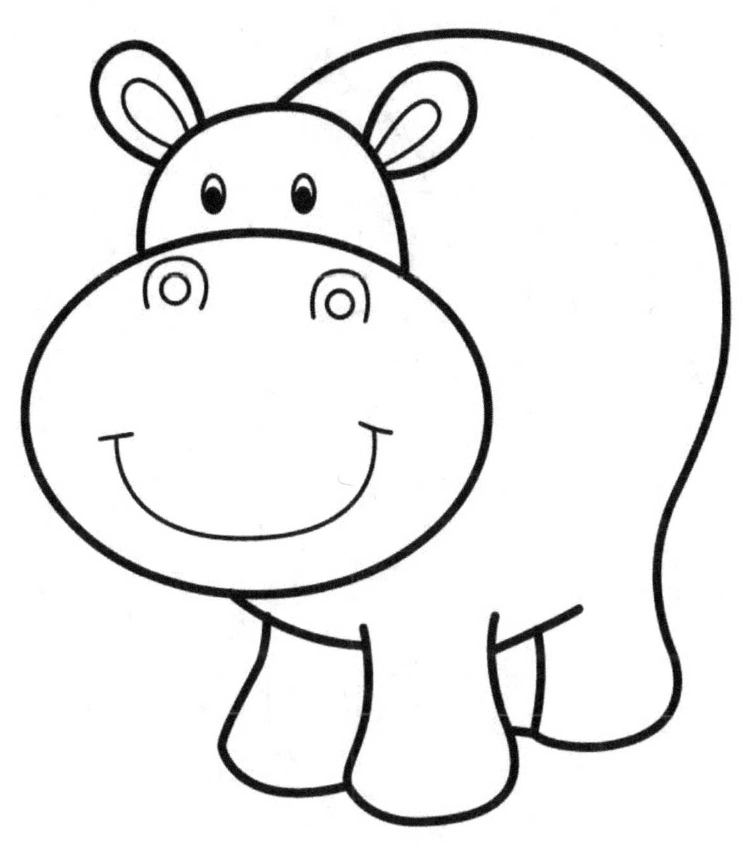

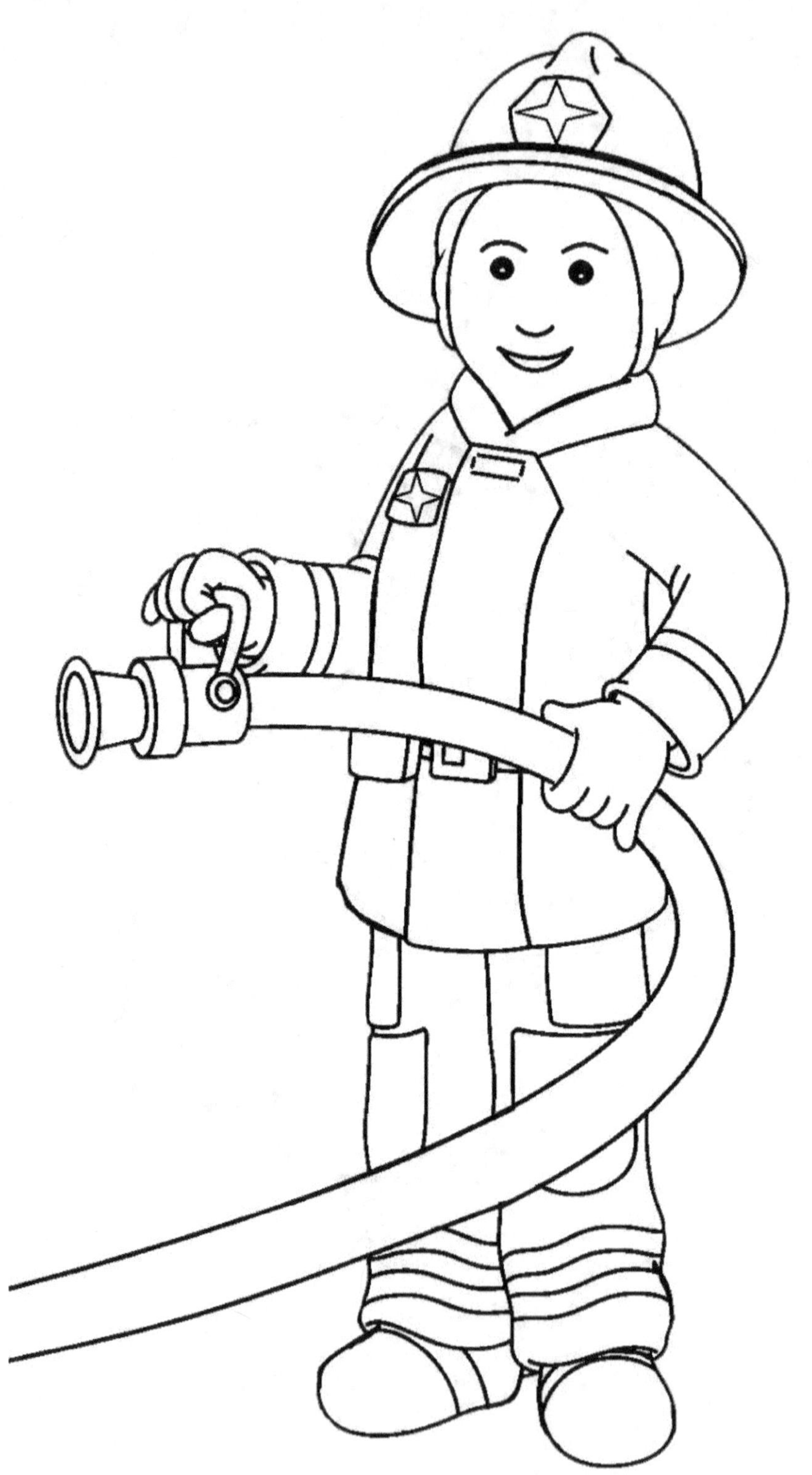

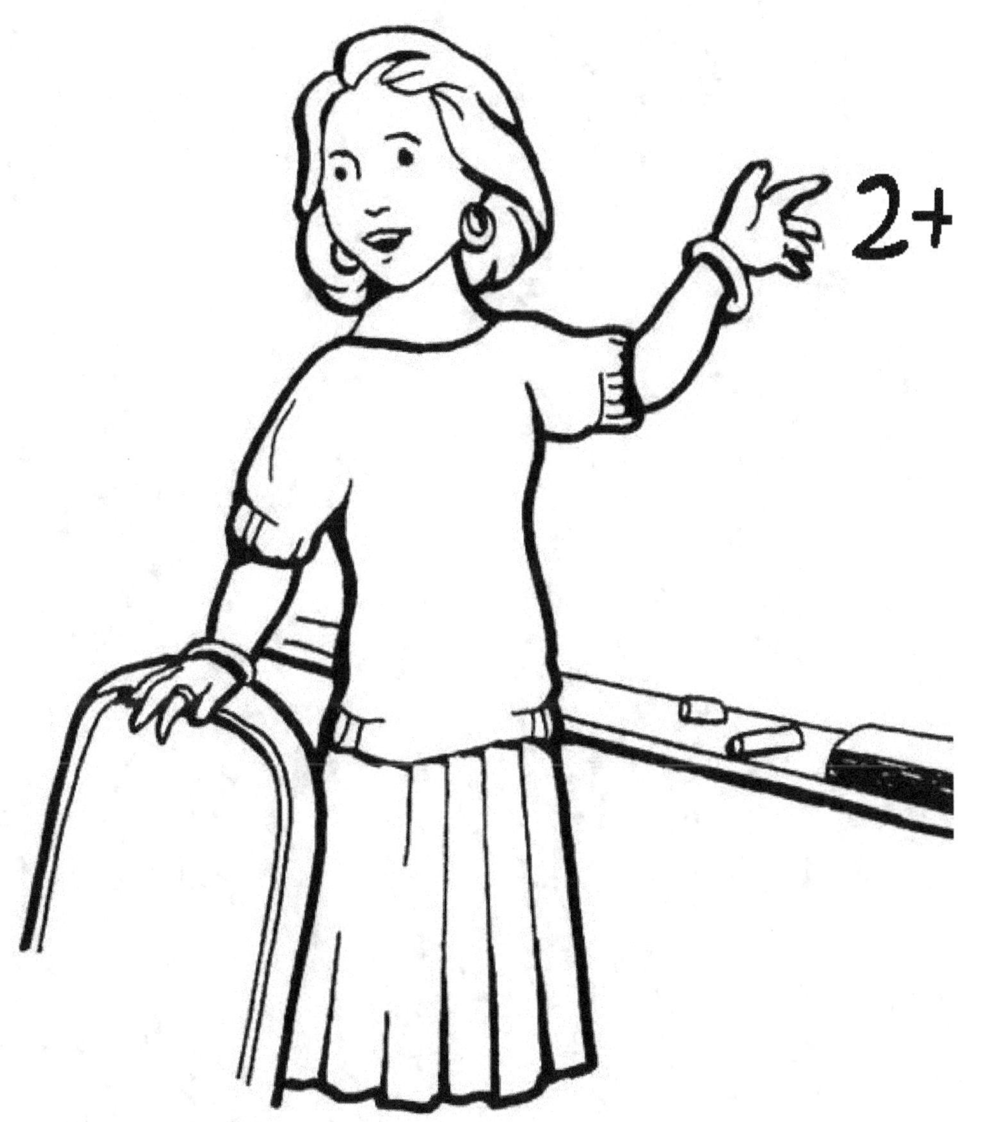
2+

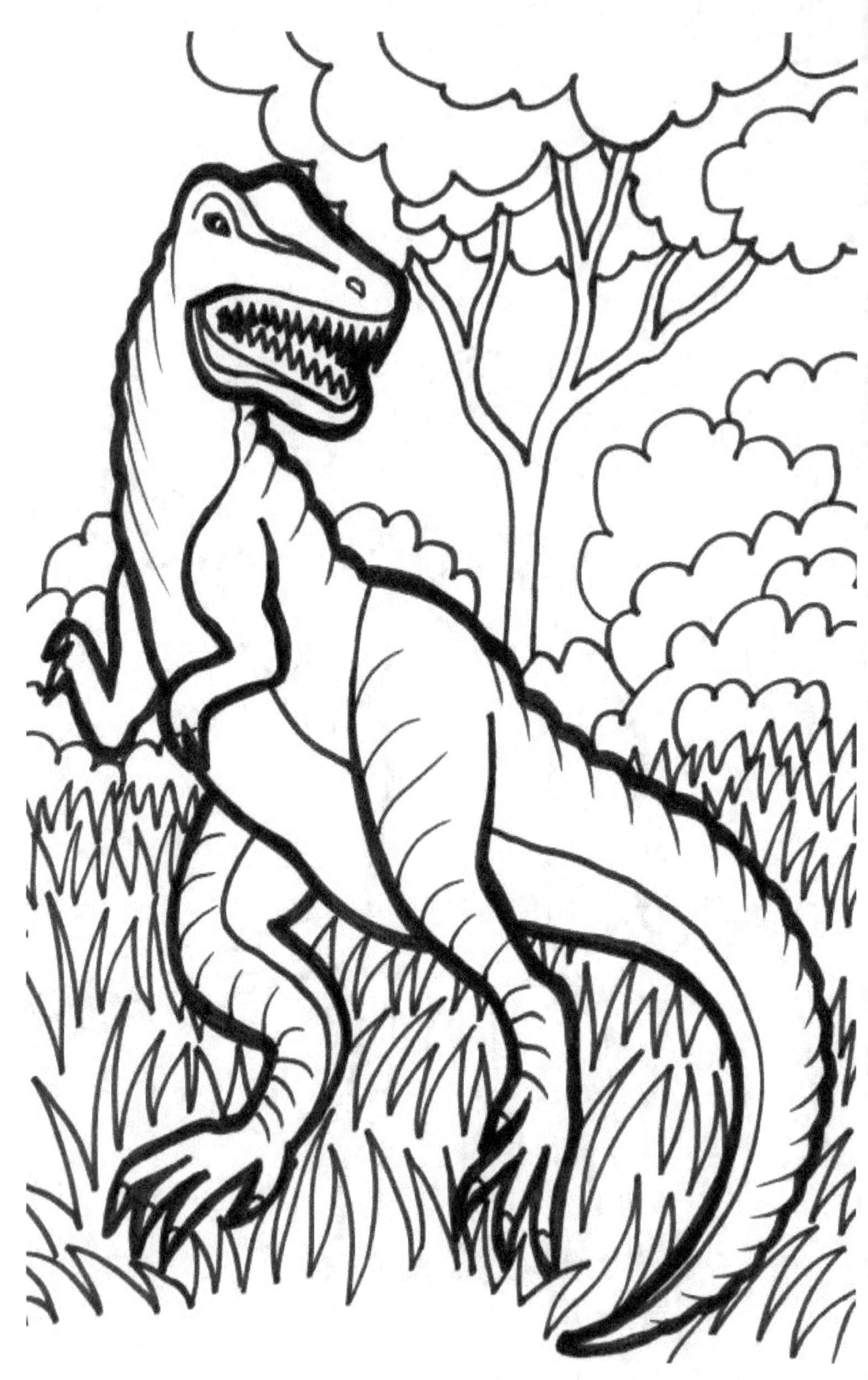

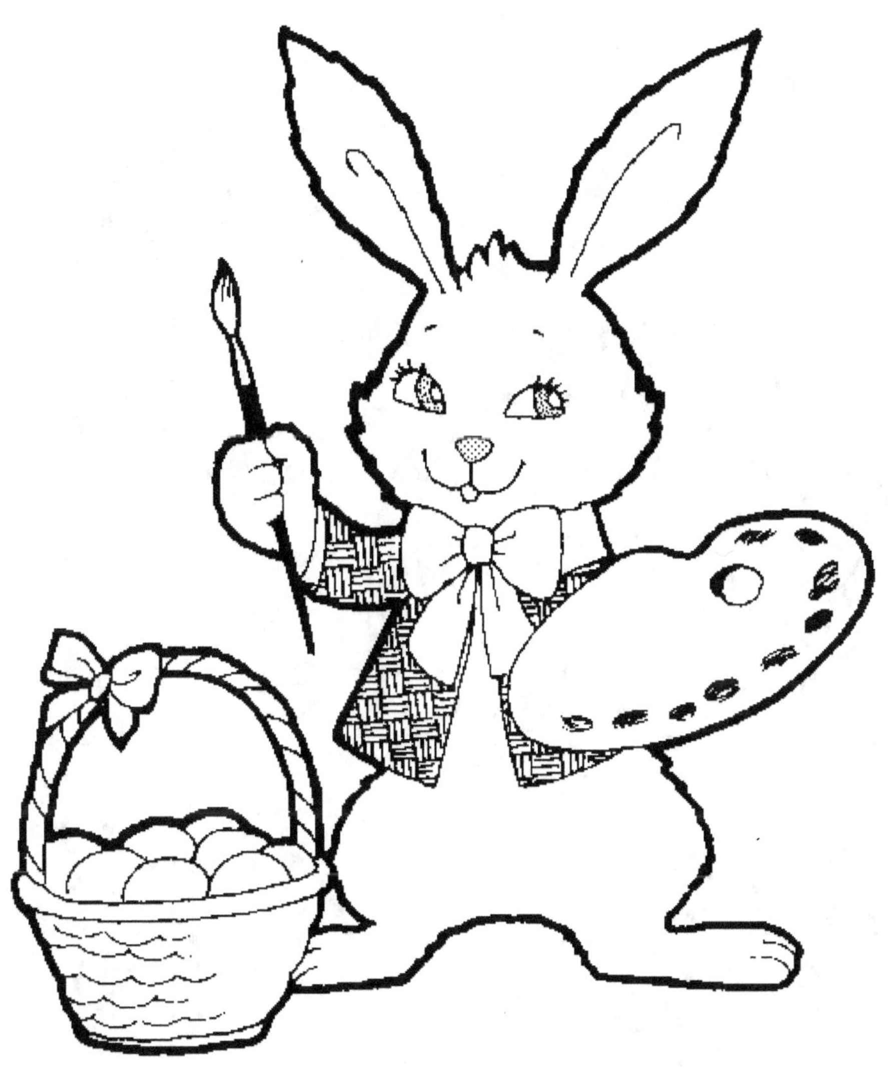

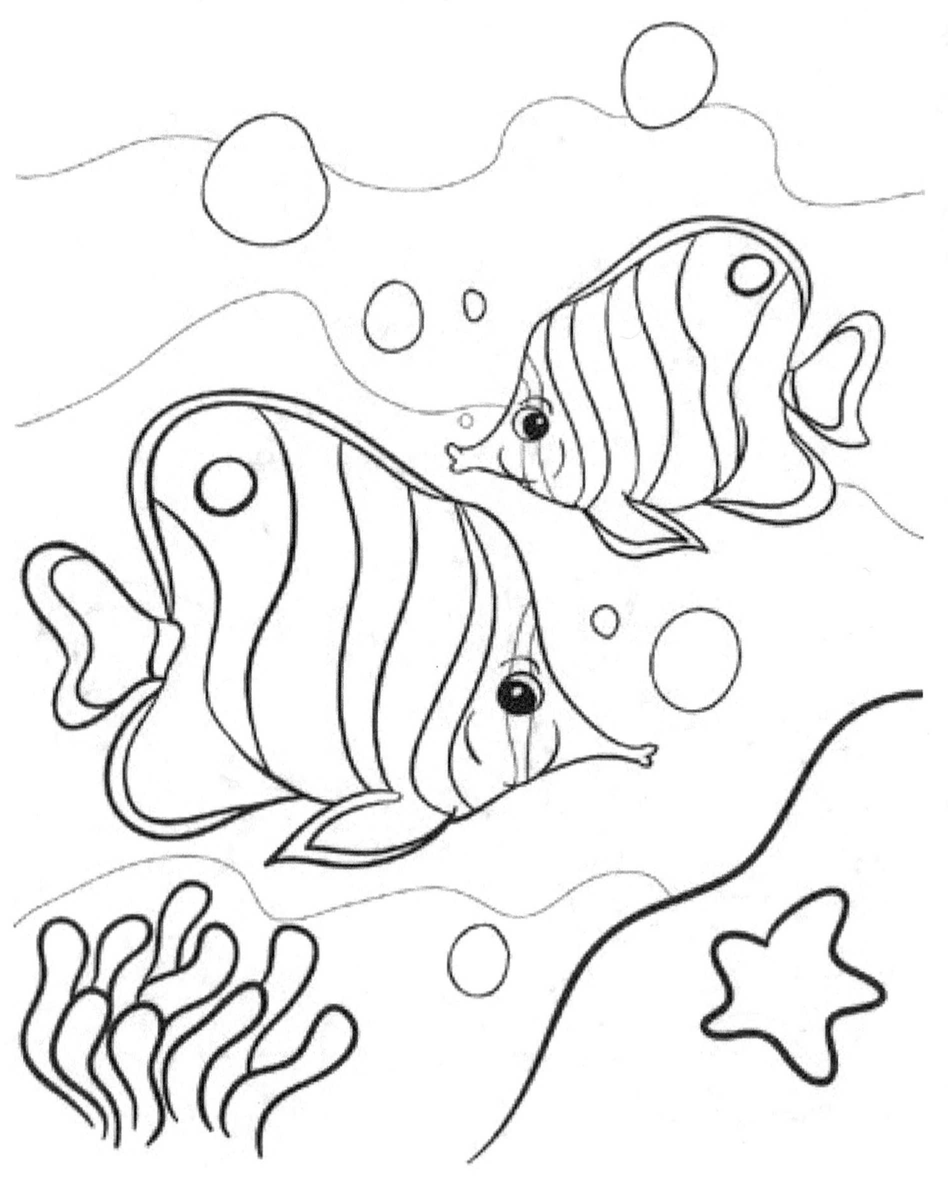

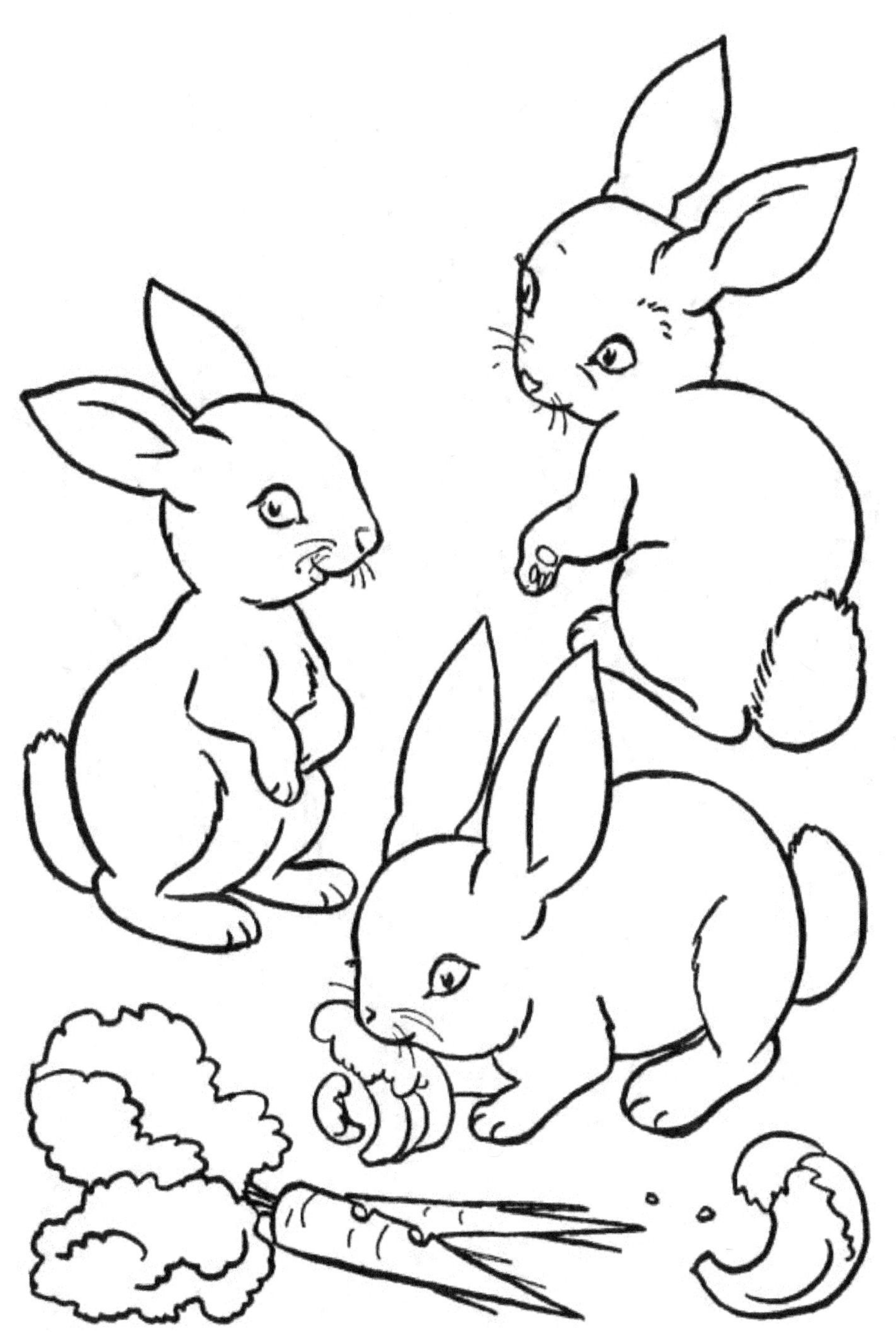

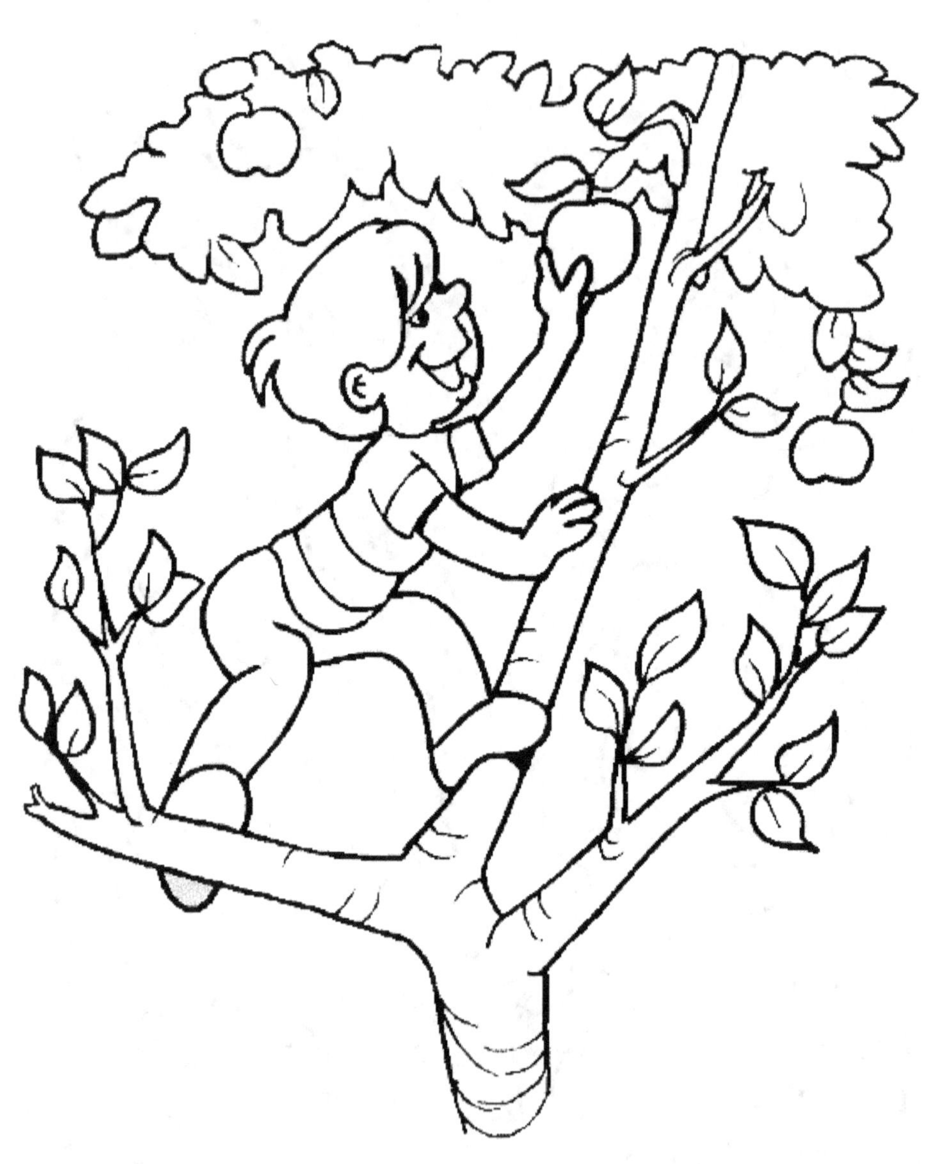

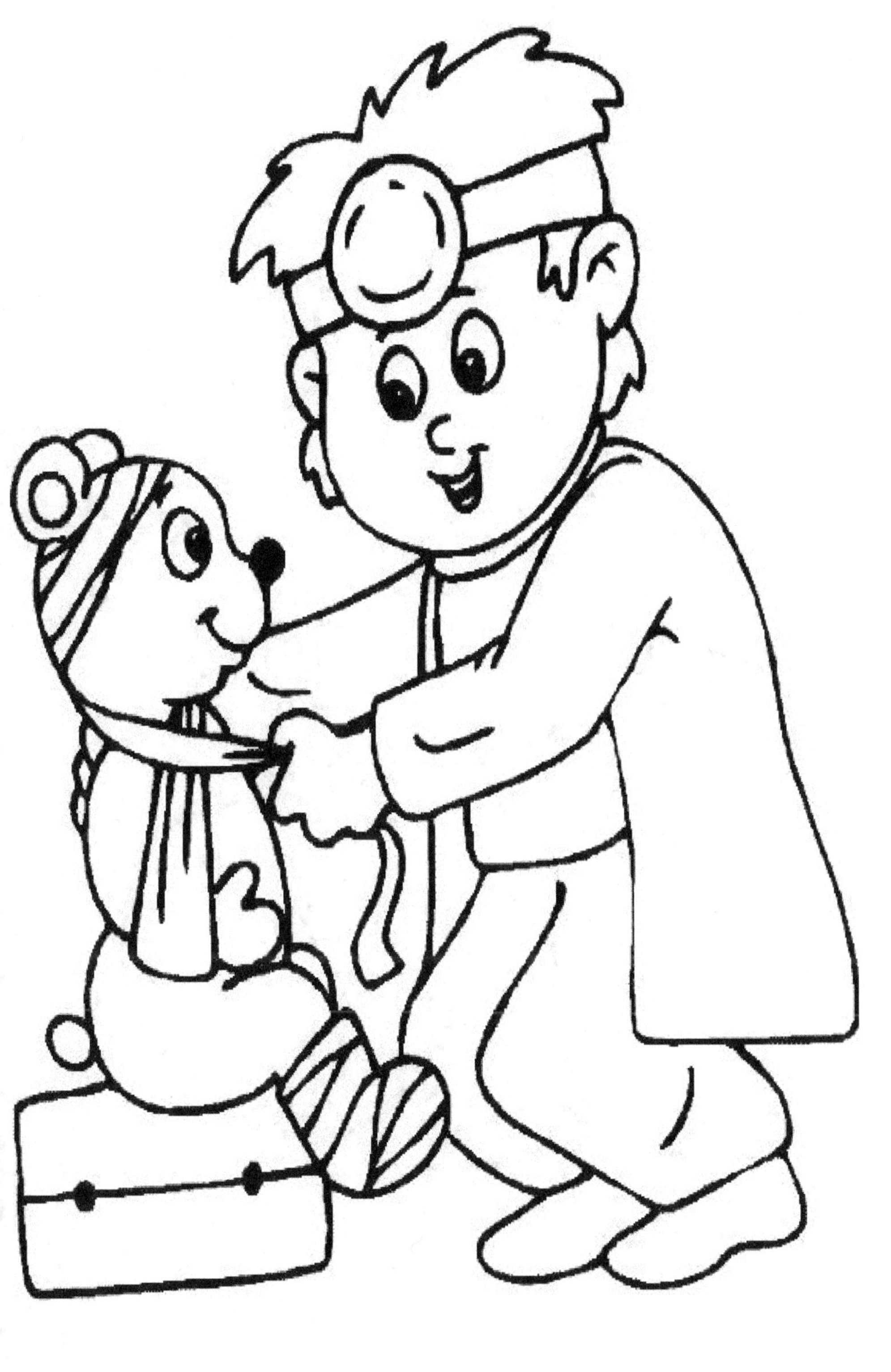

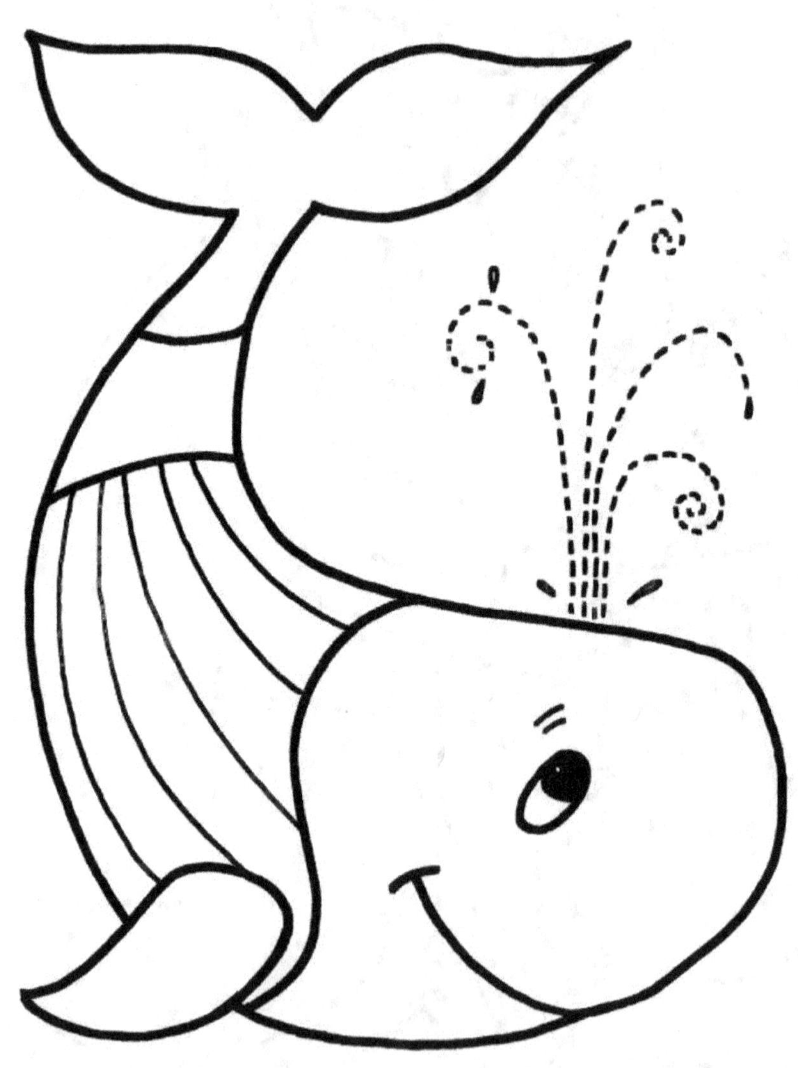

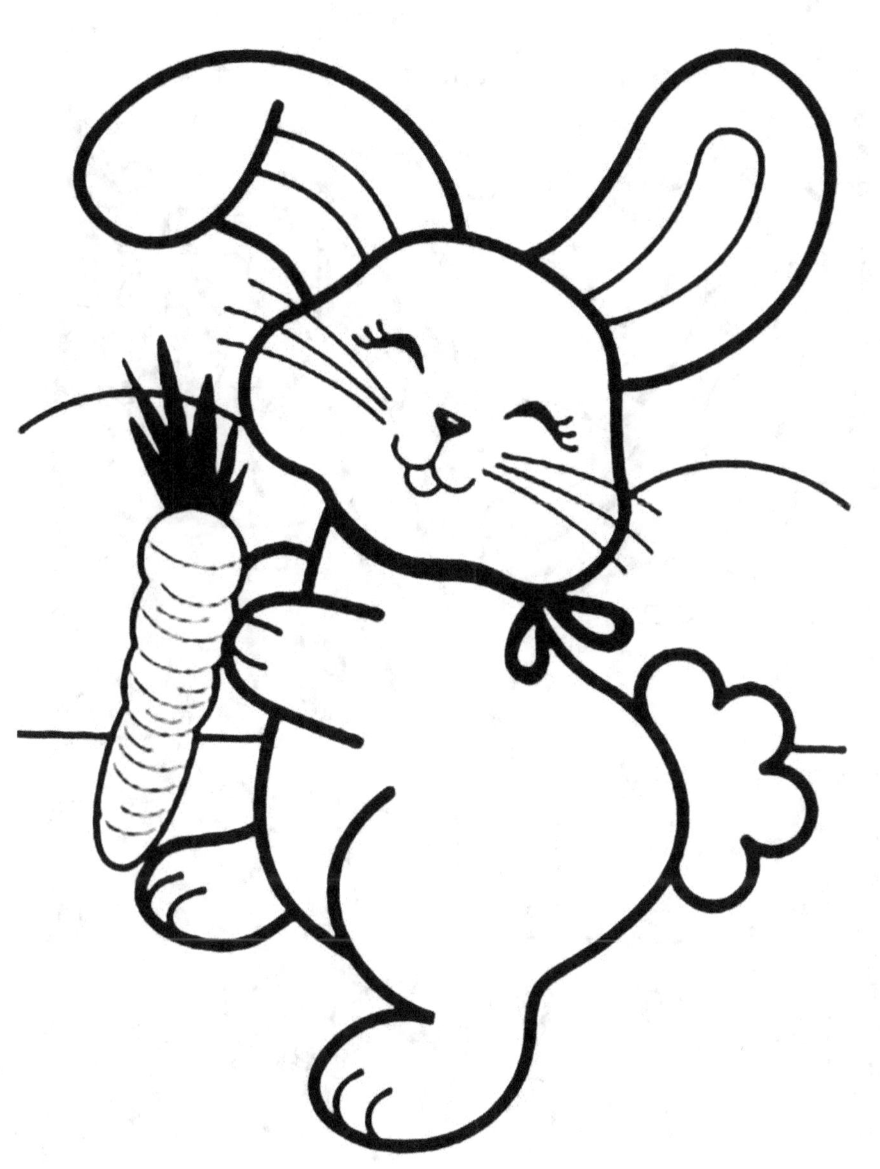

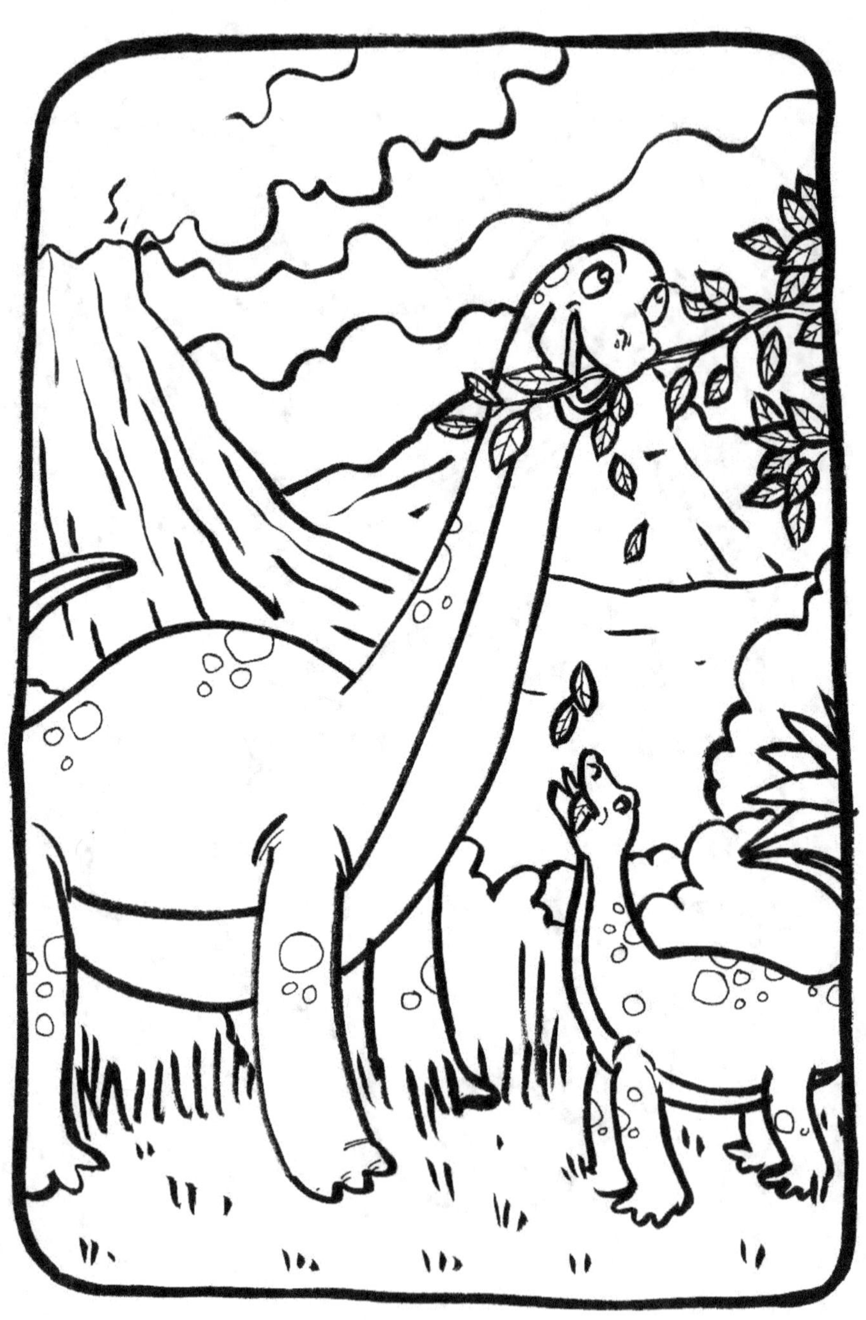

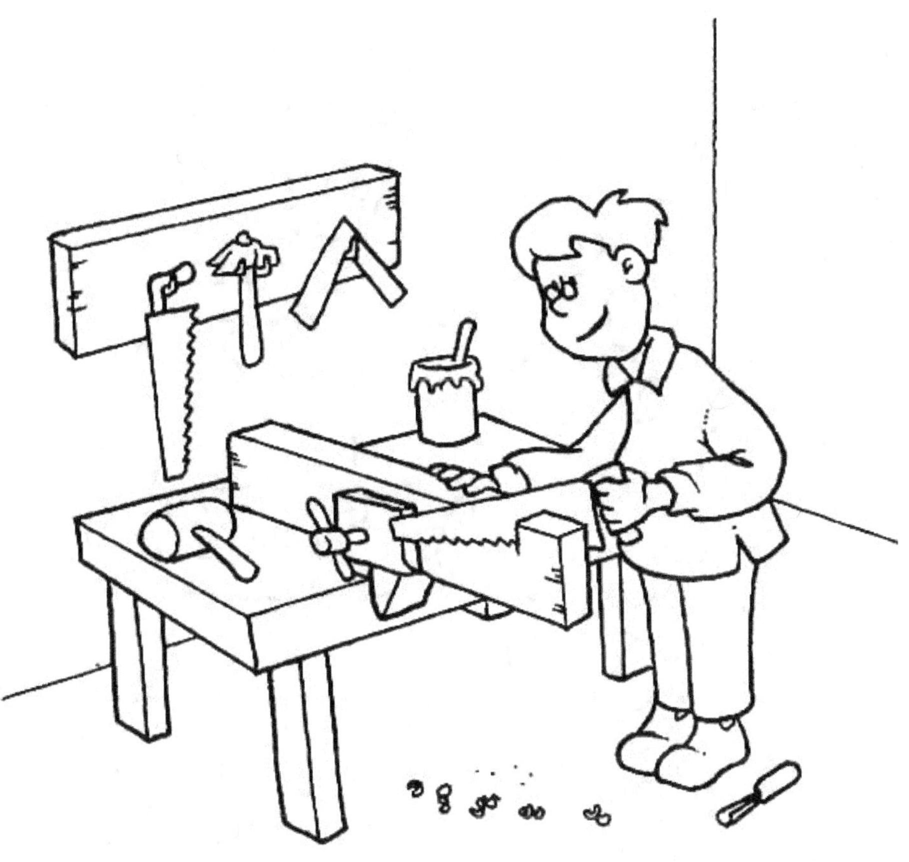

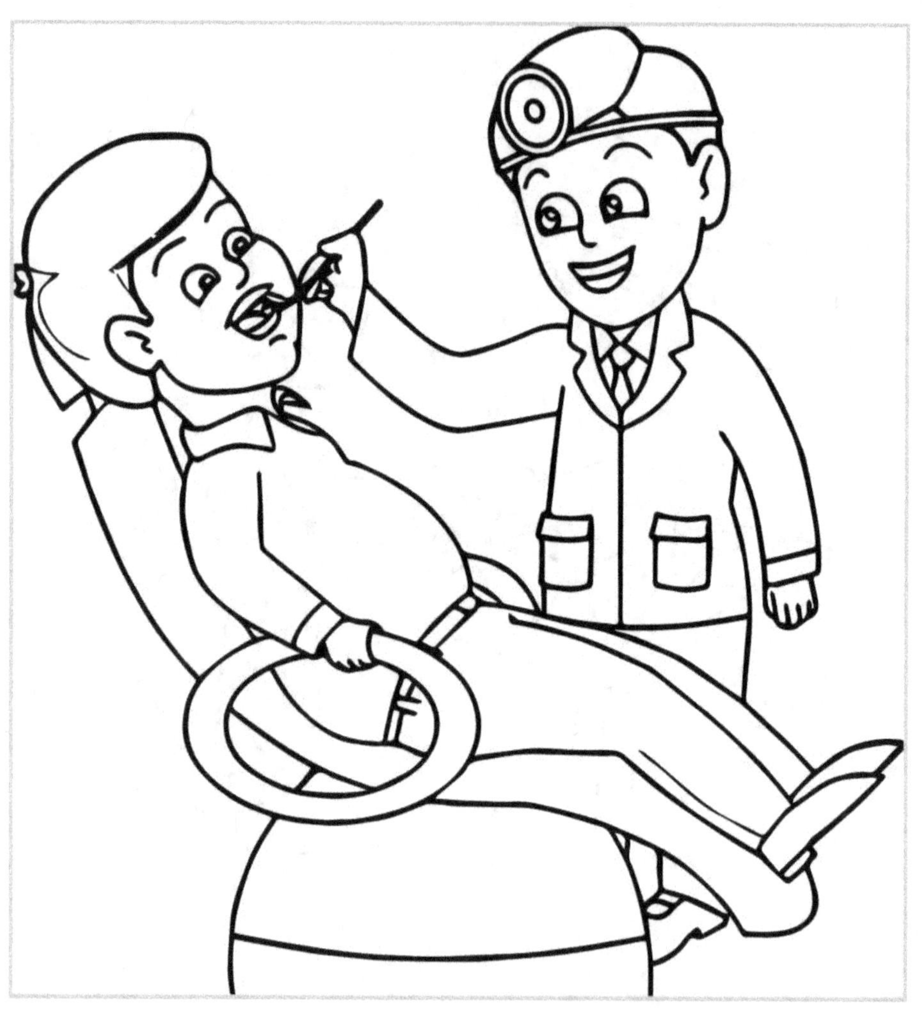

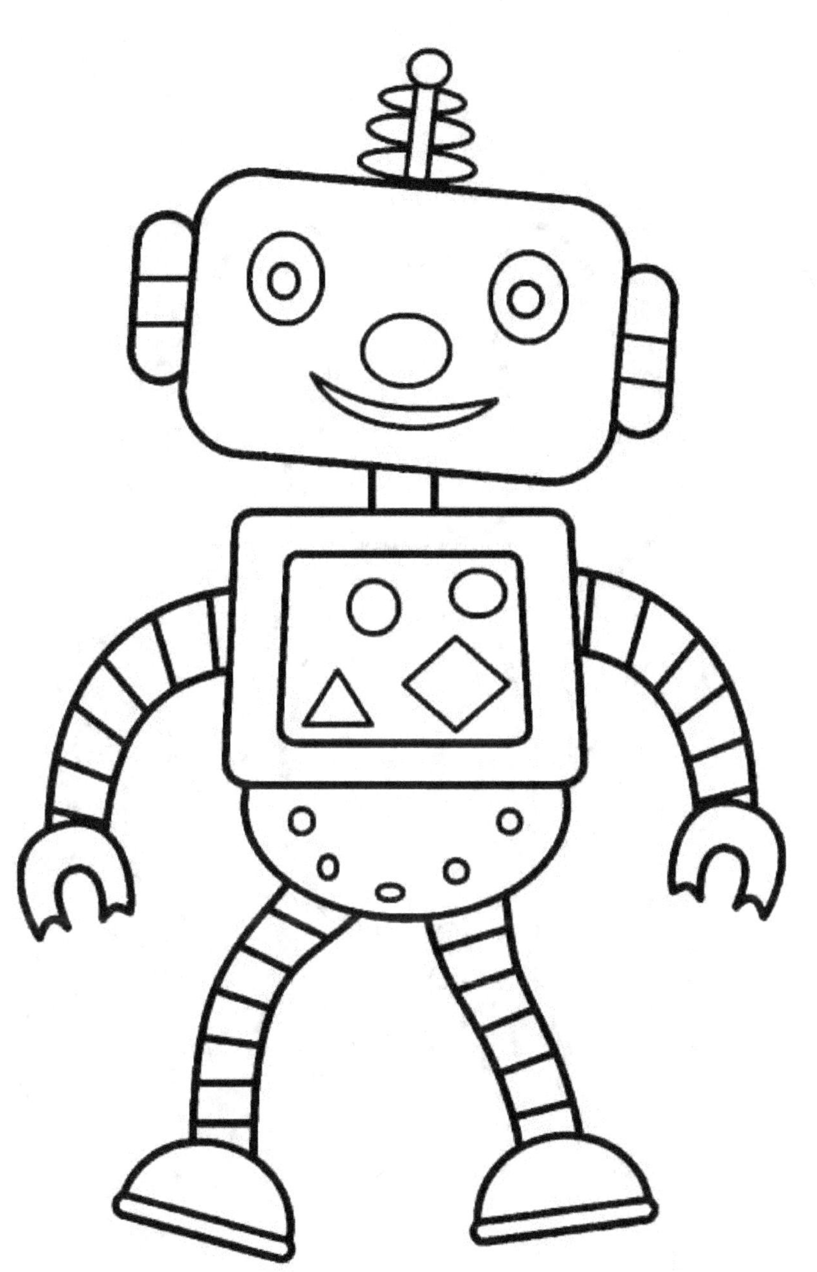

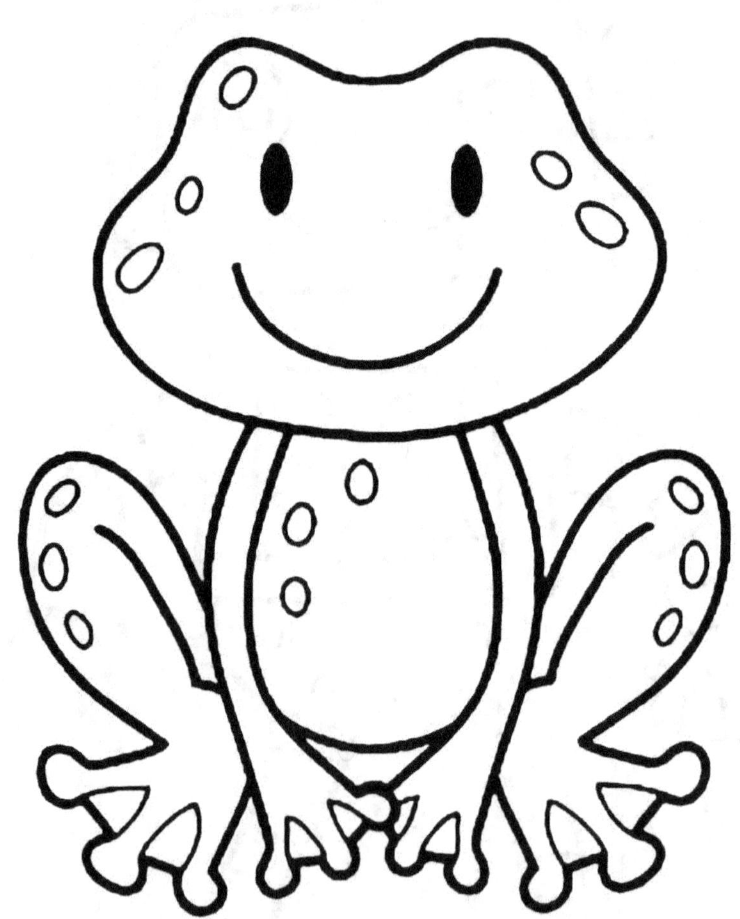

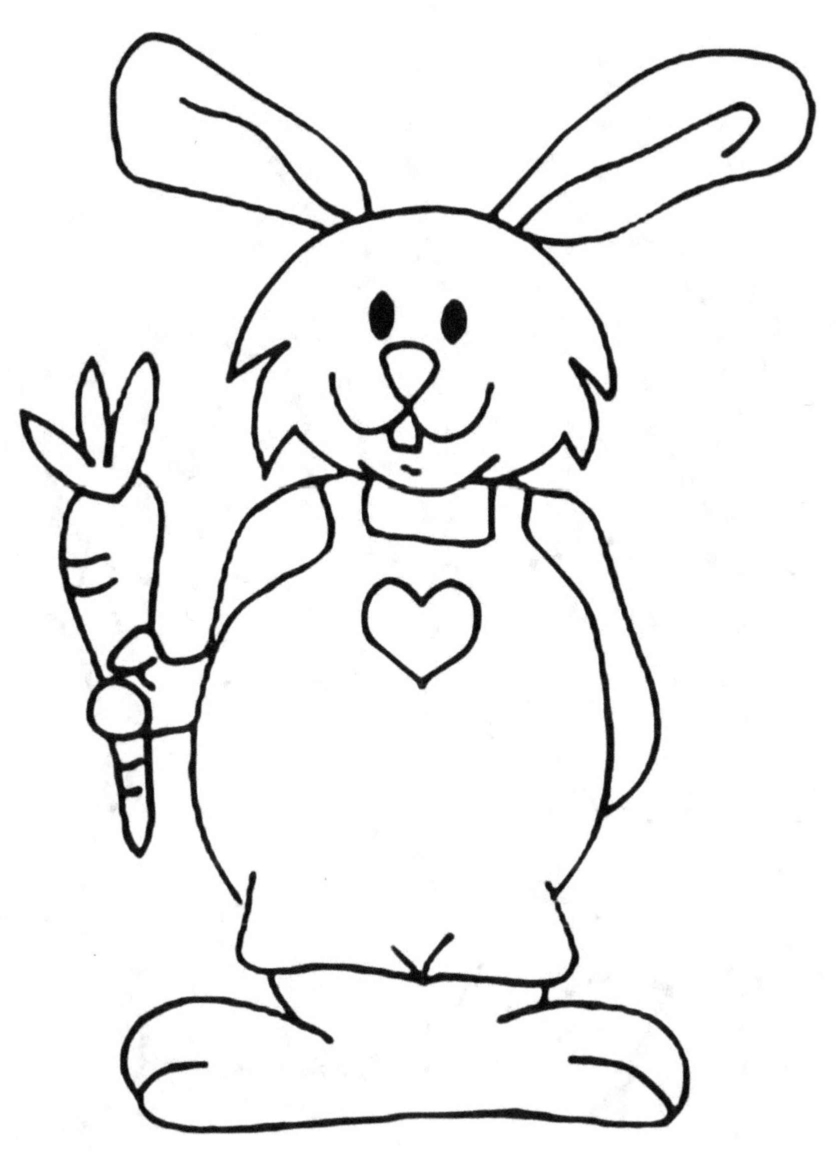

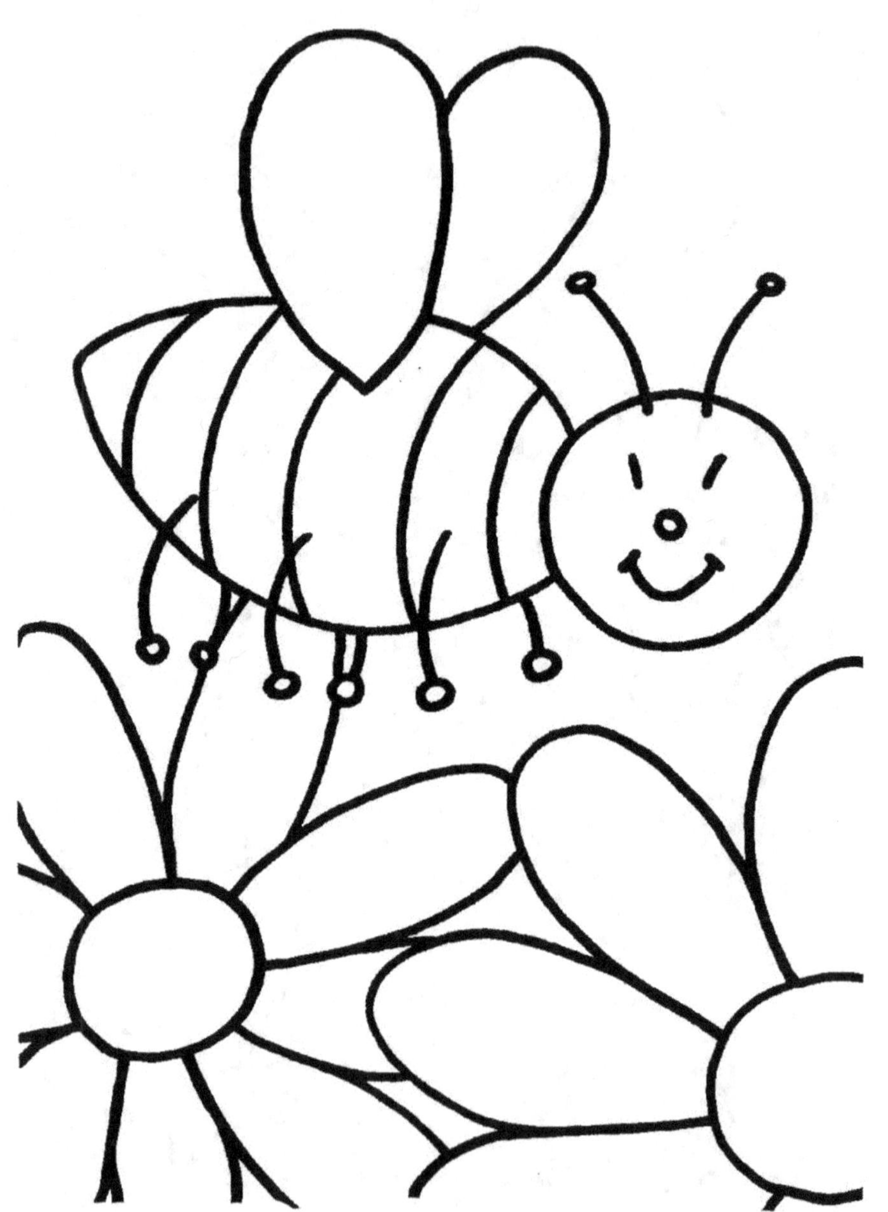

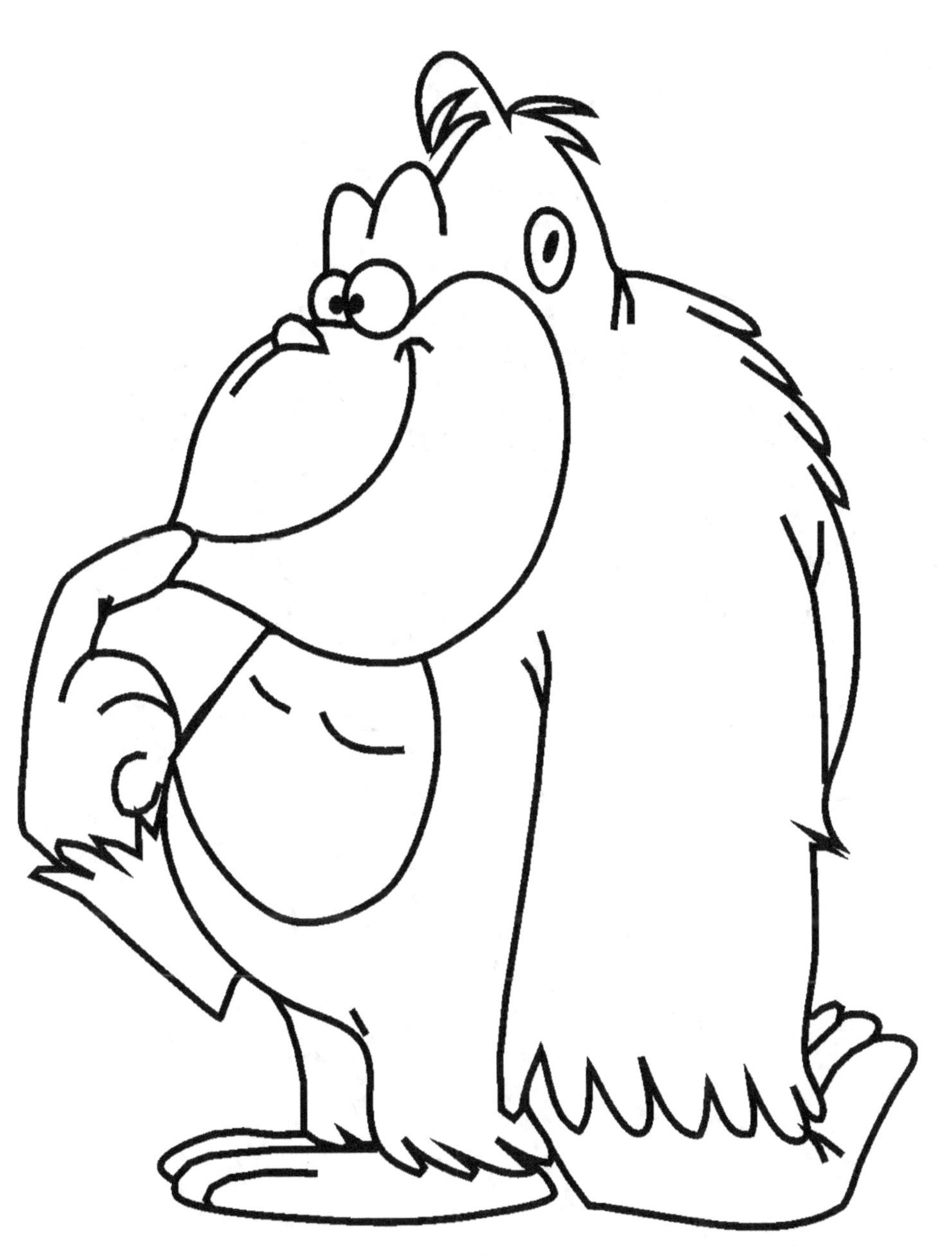

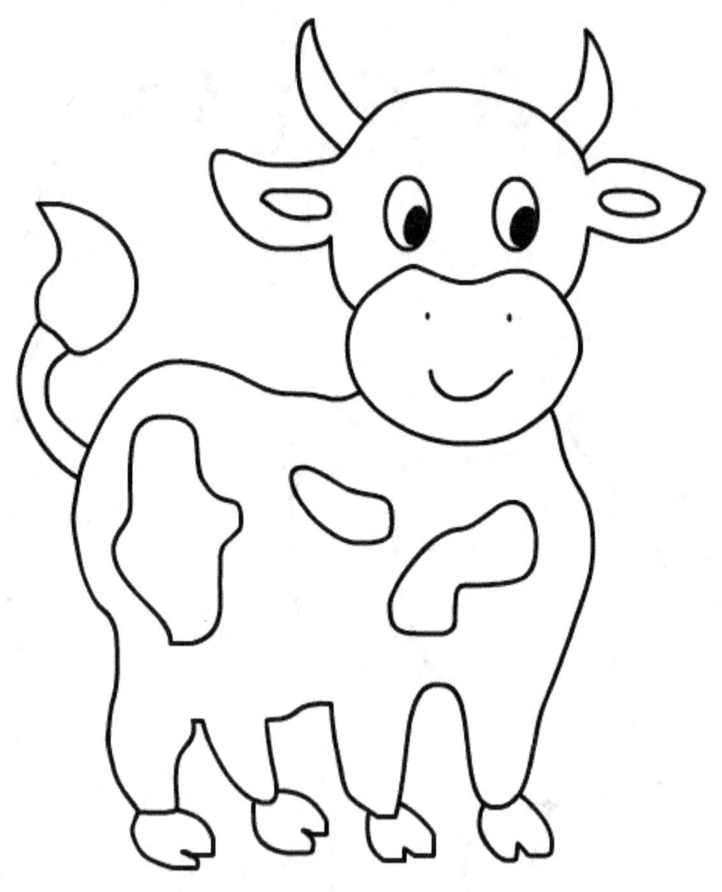

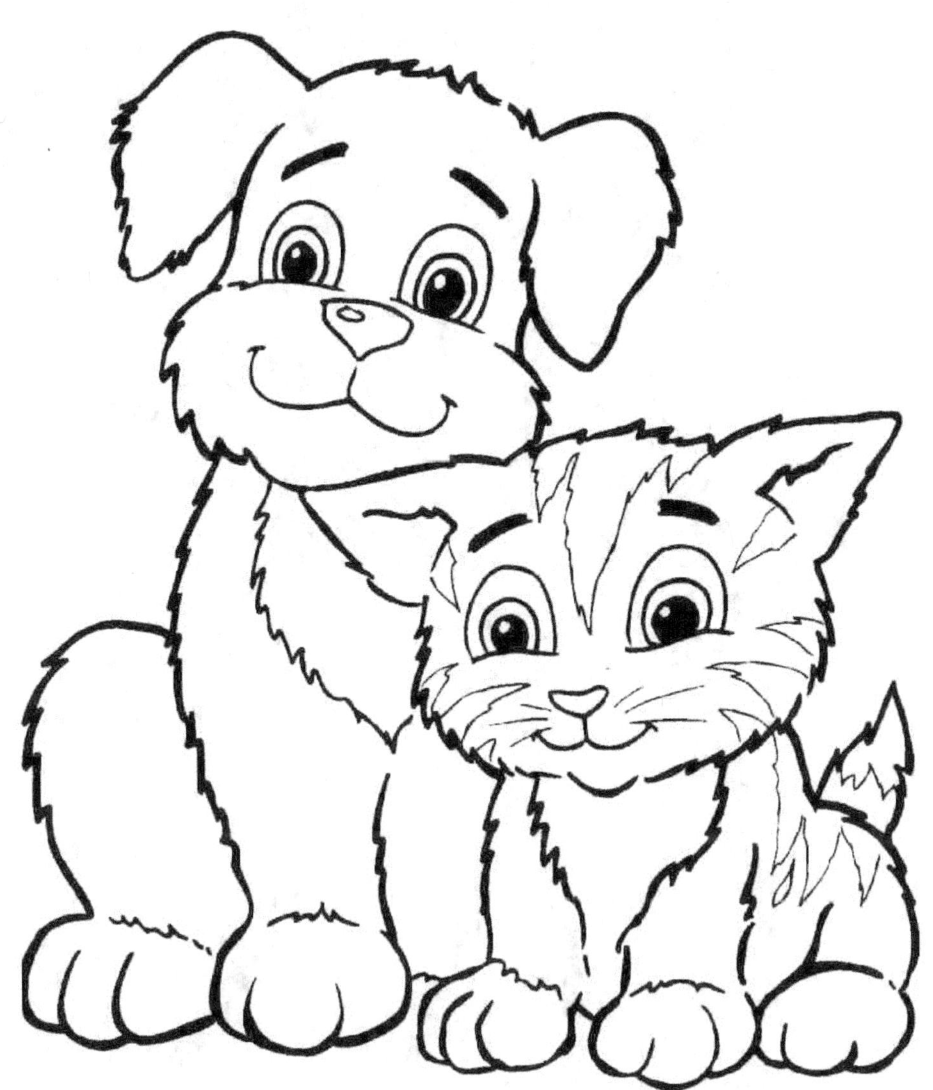

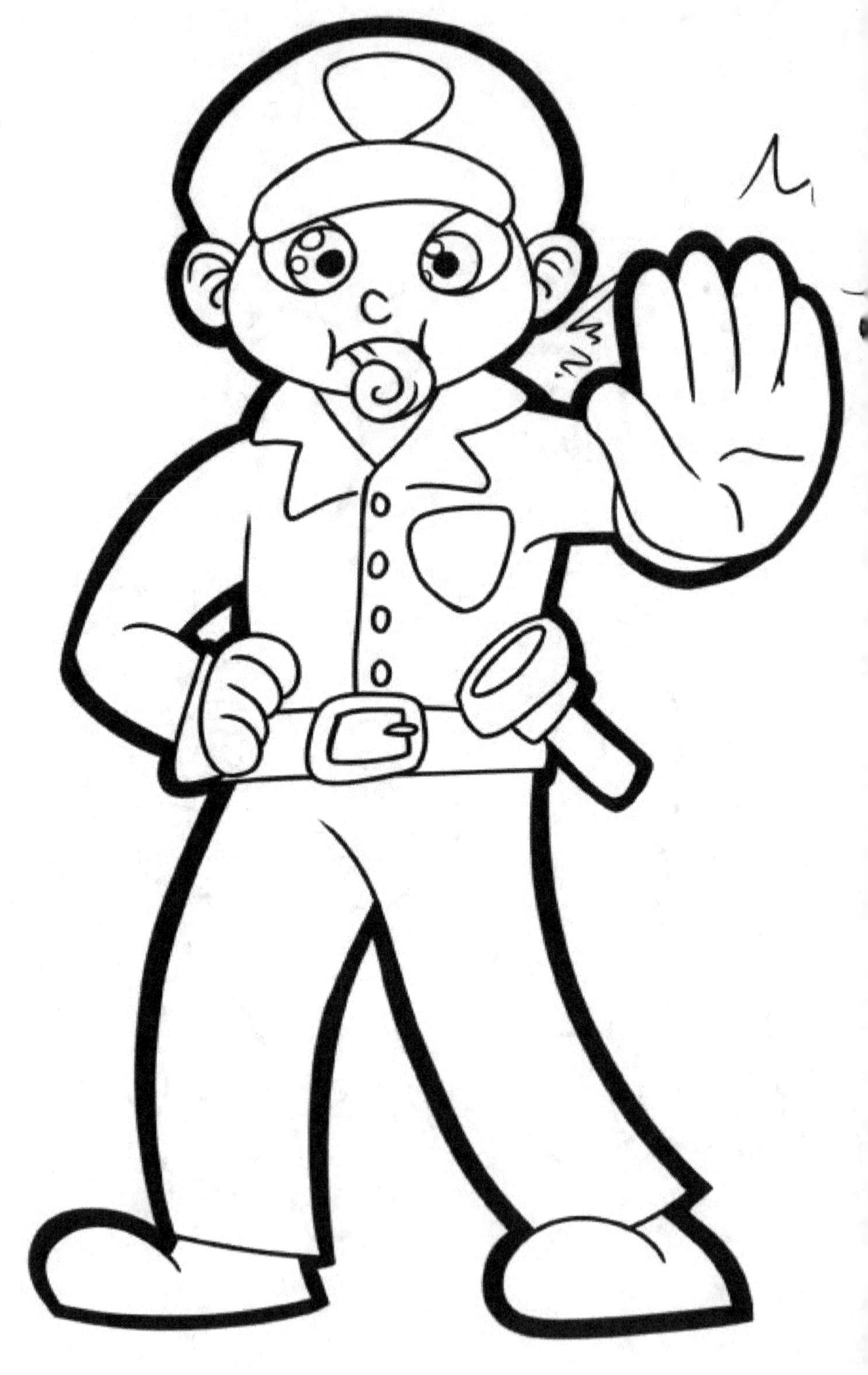

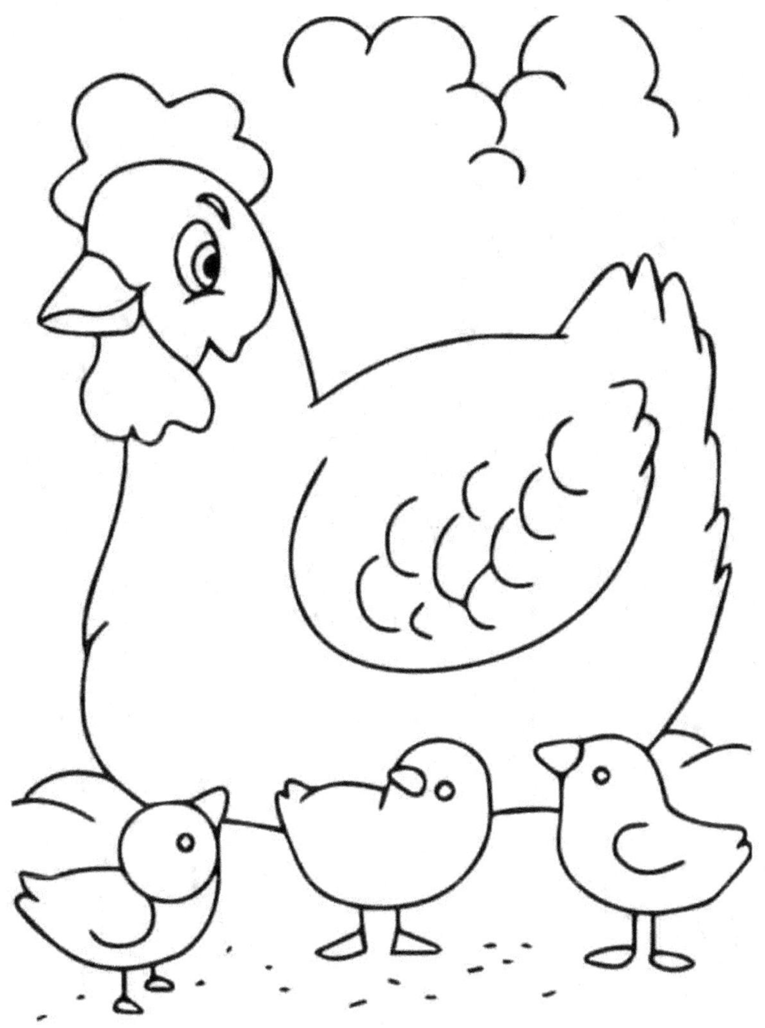

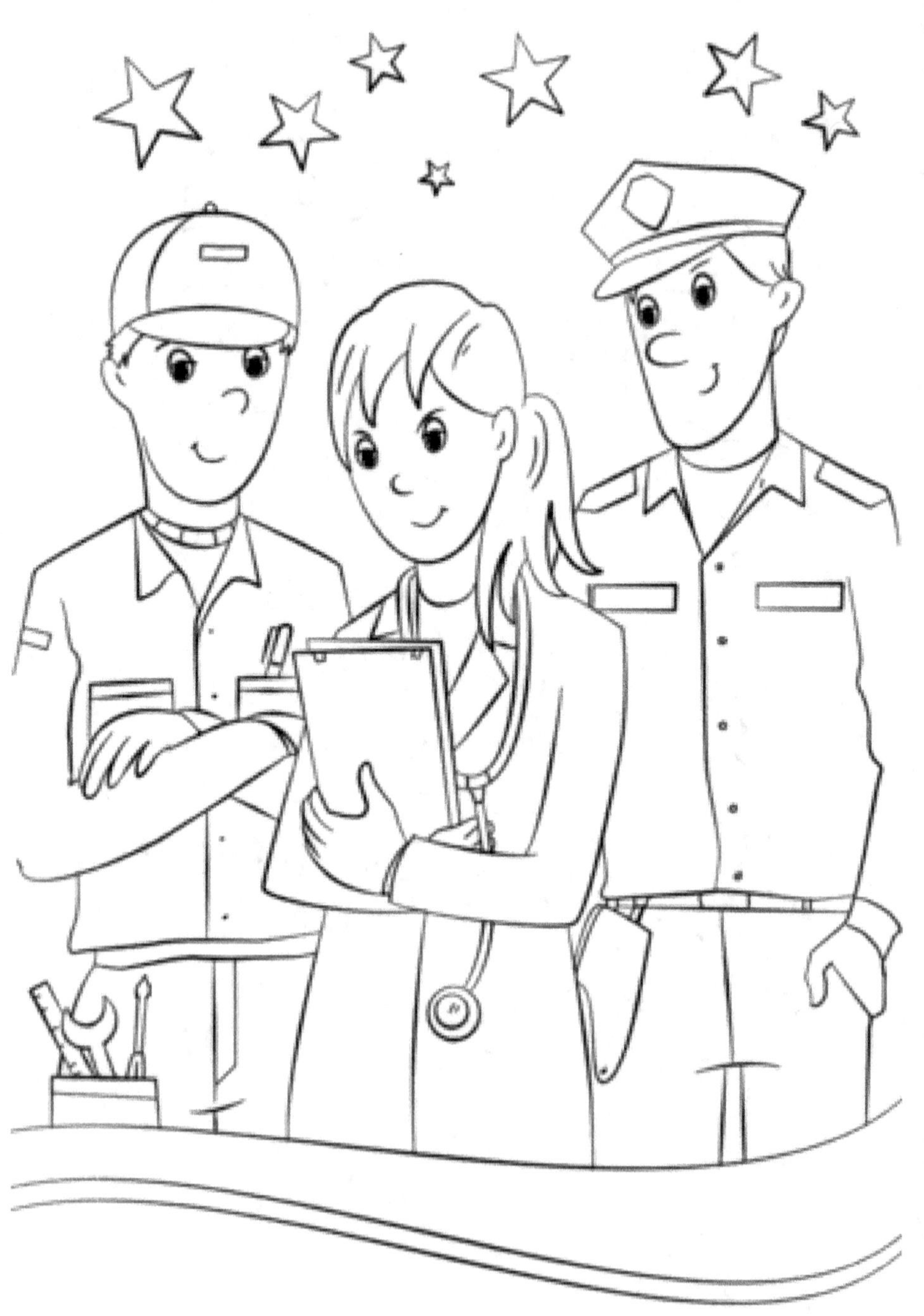

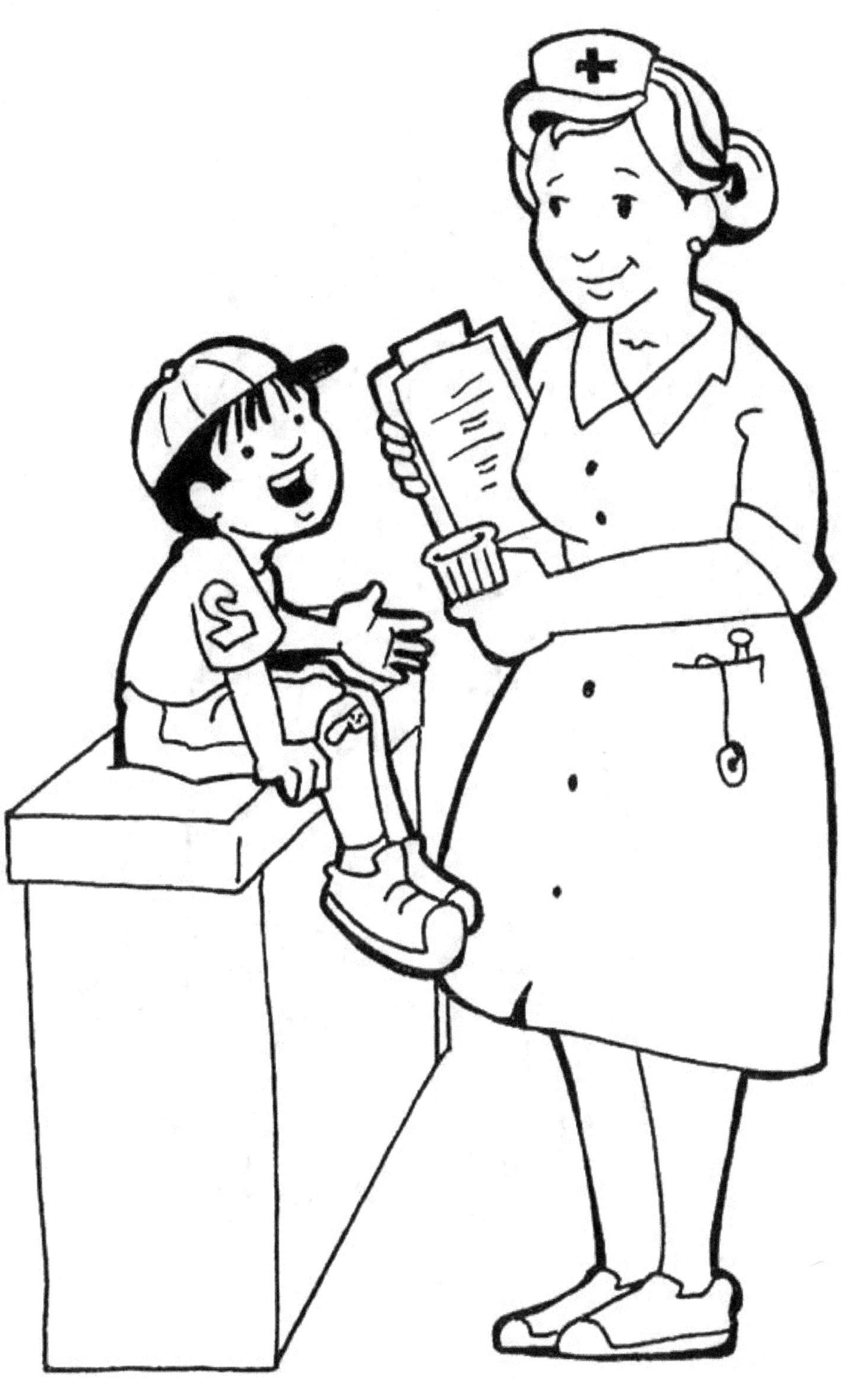

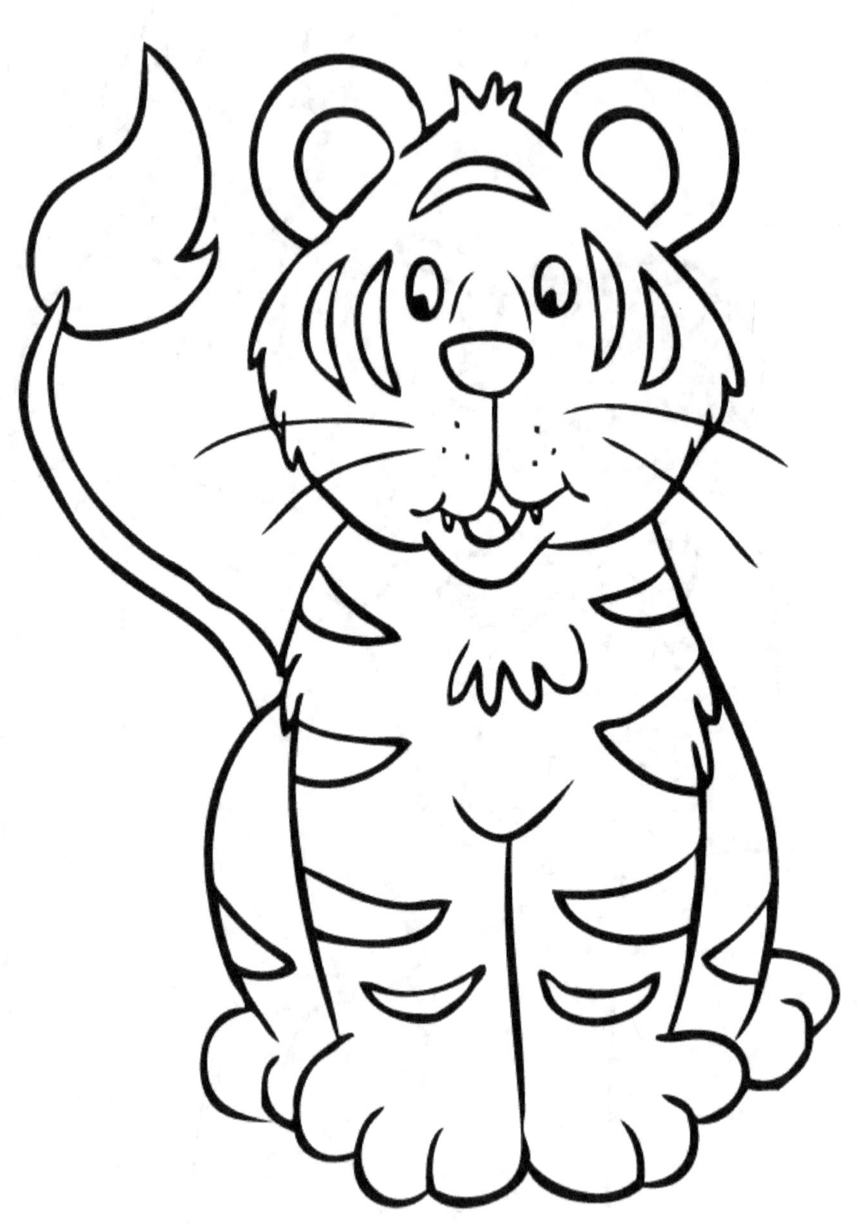

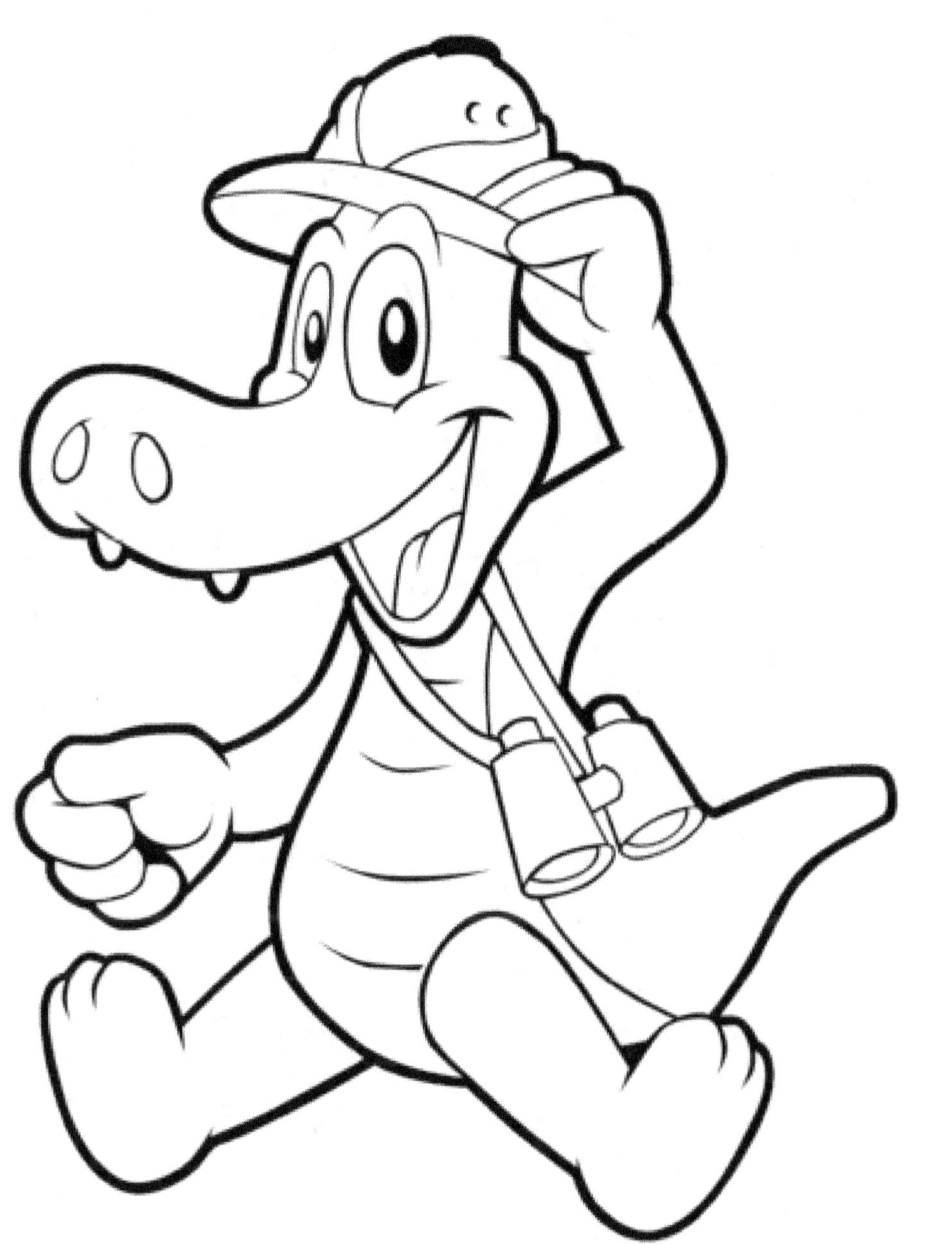

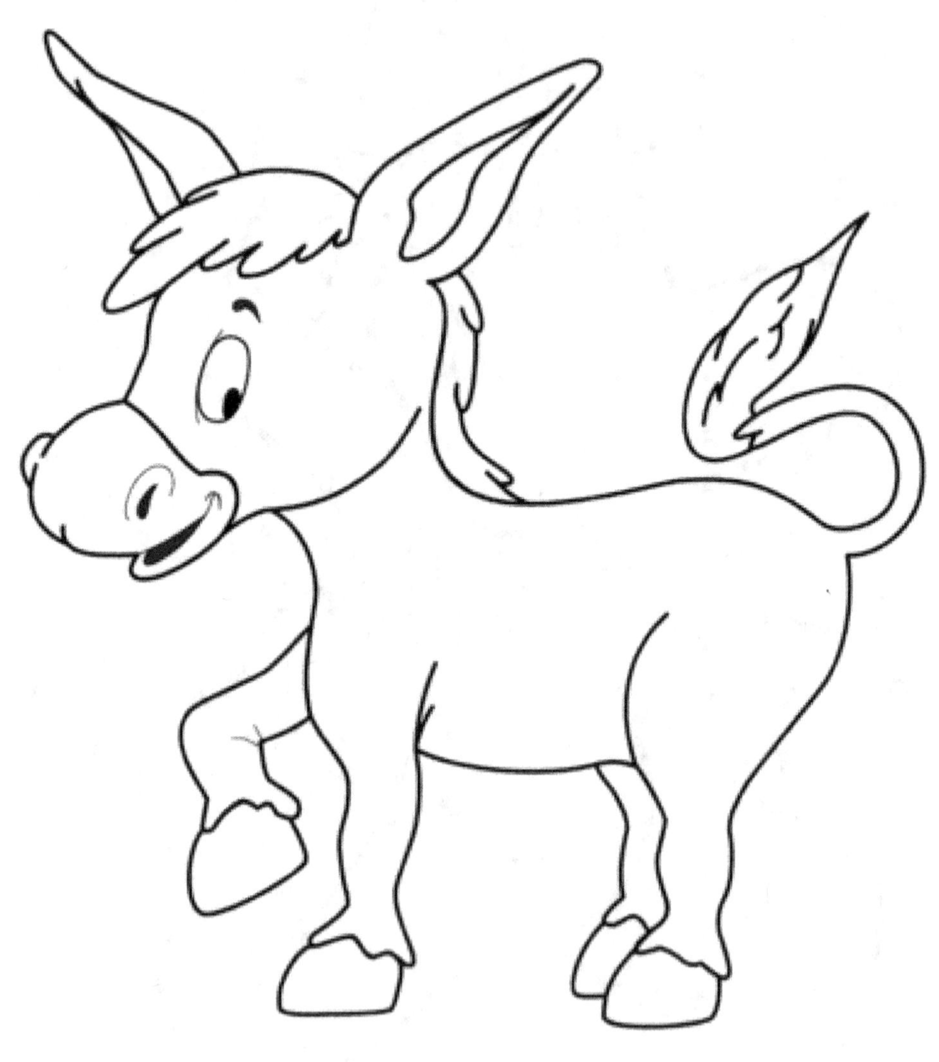

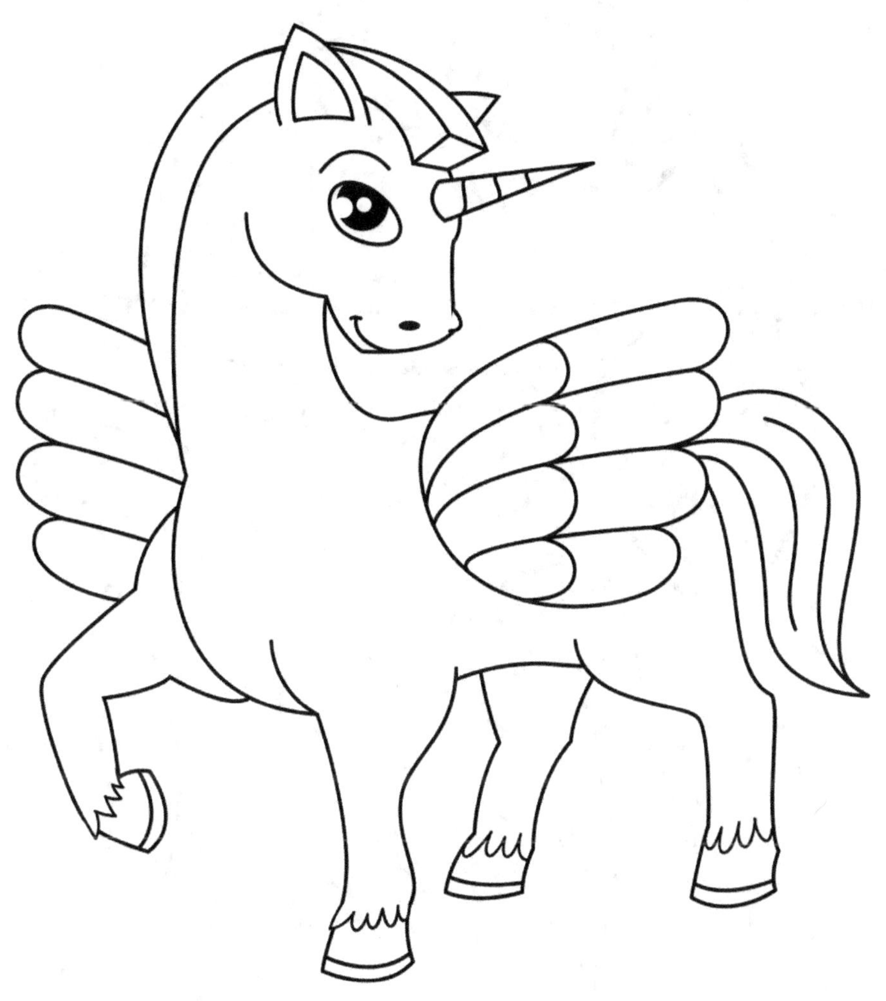

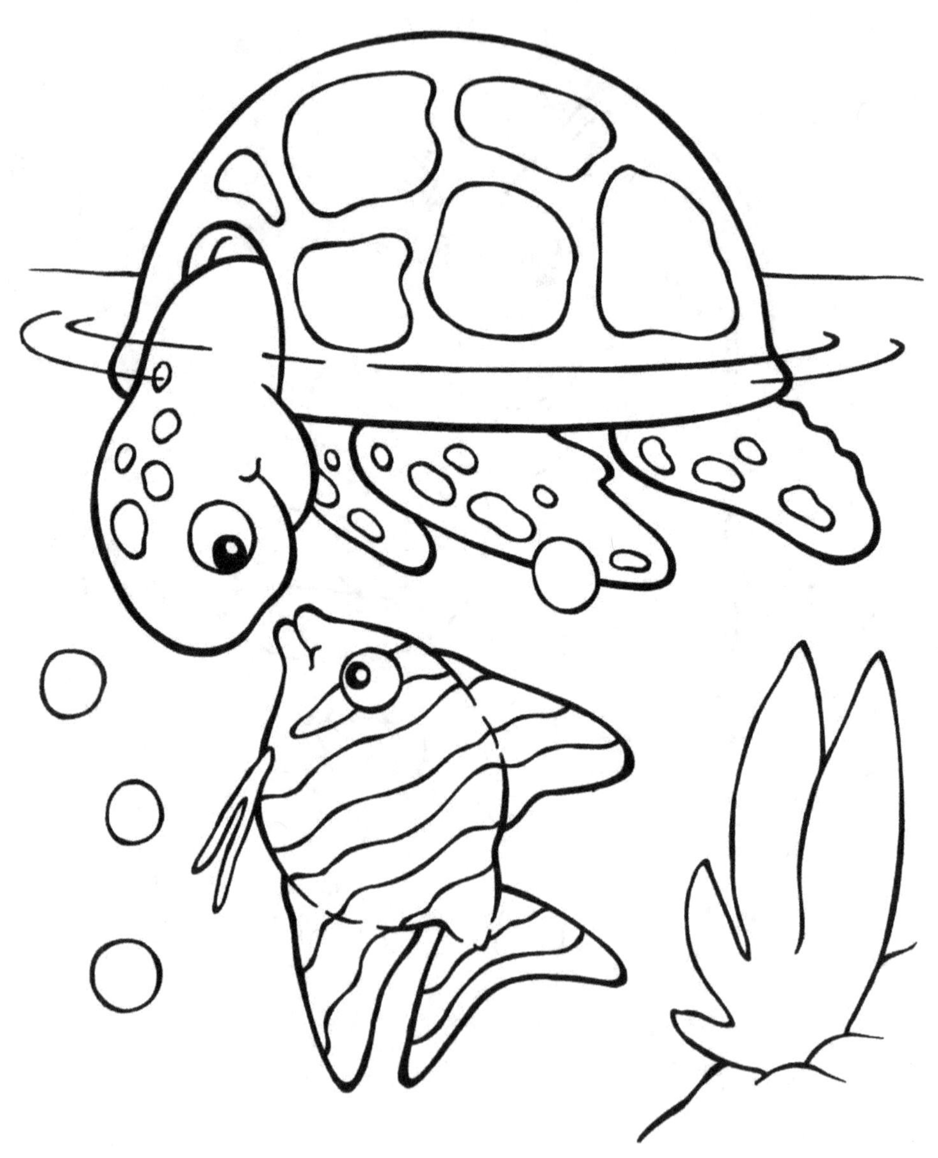

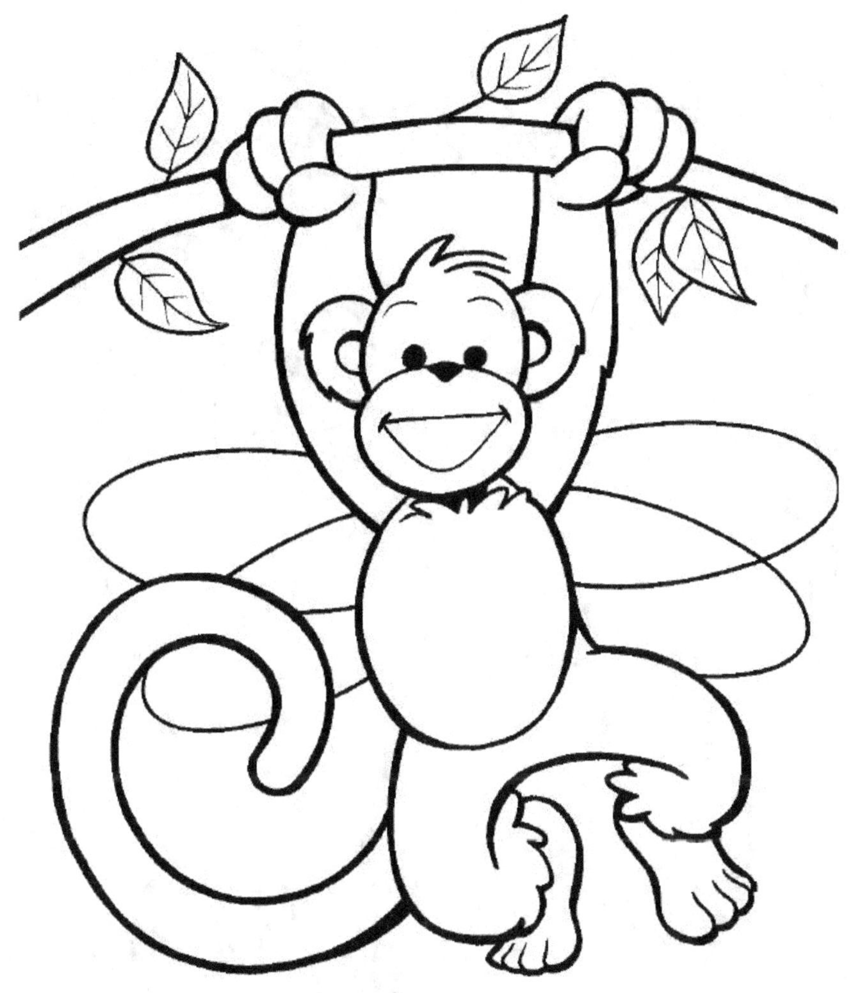

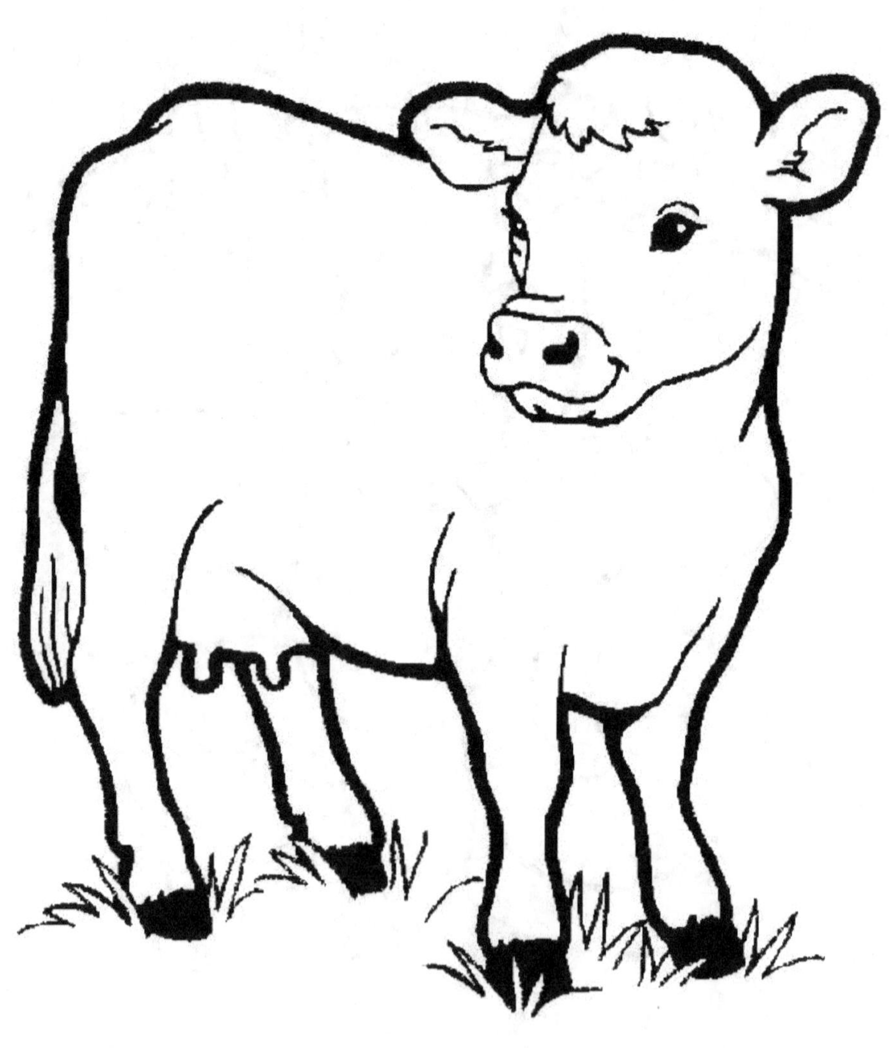

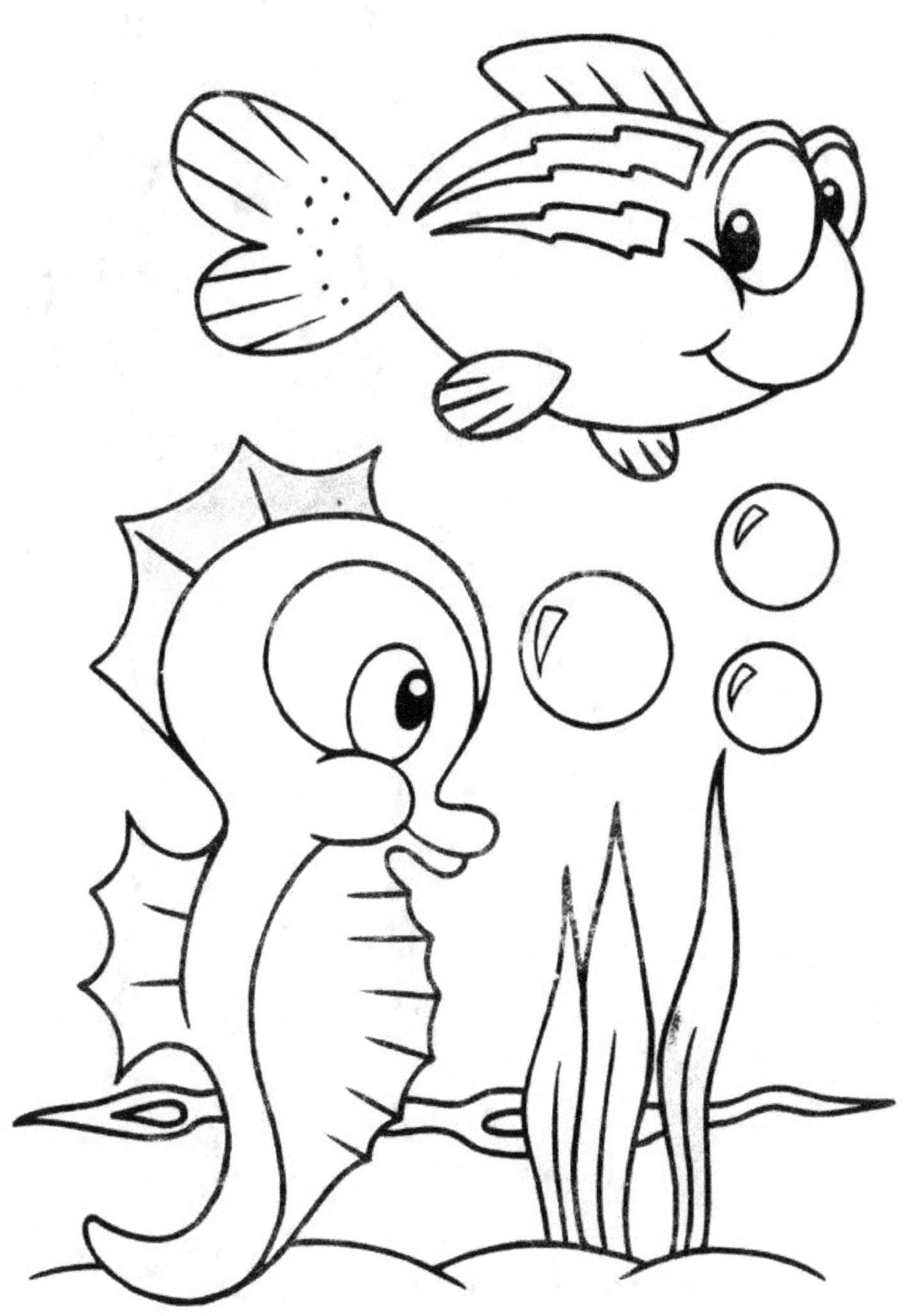

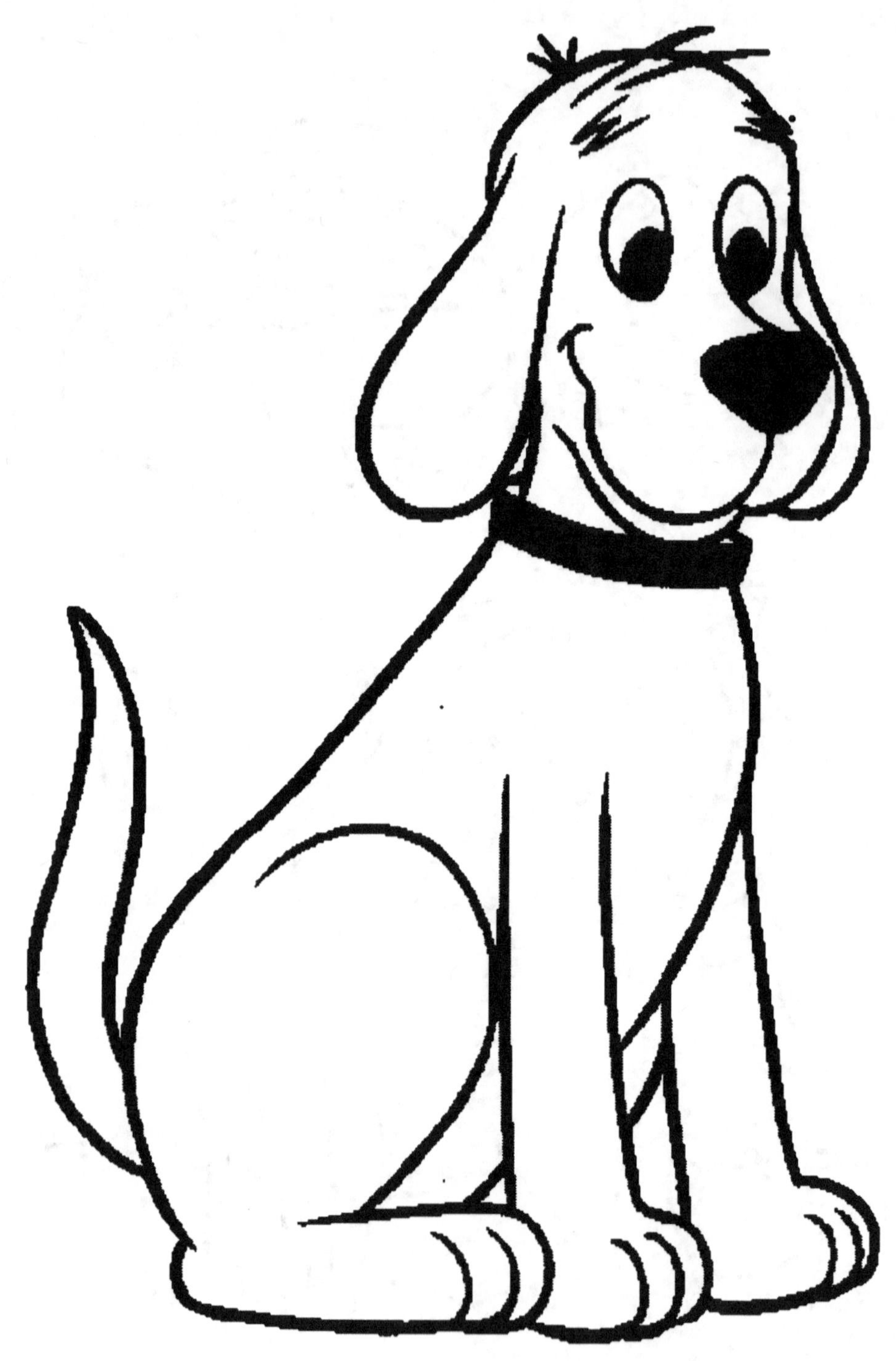

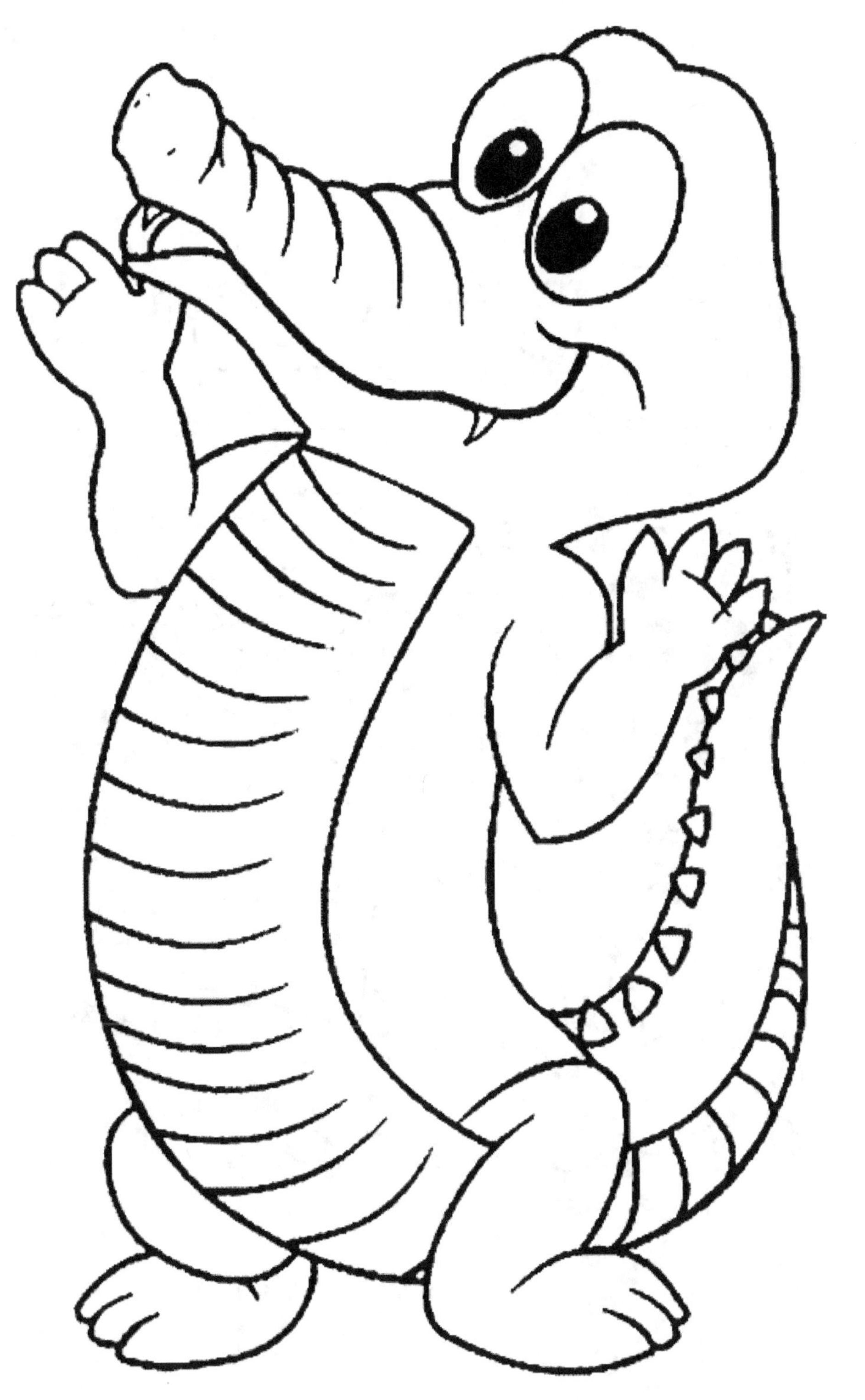

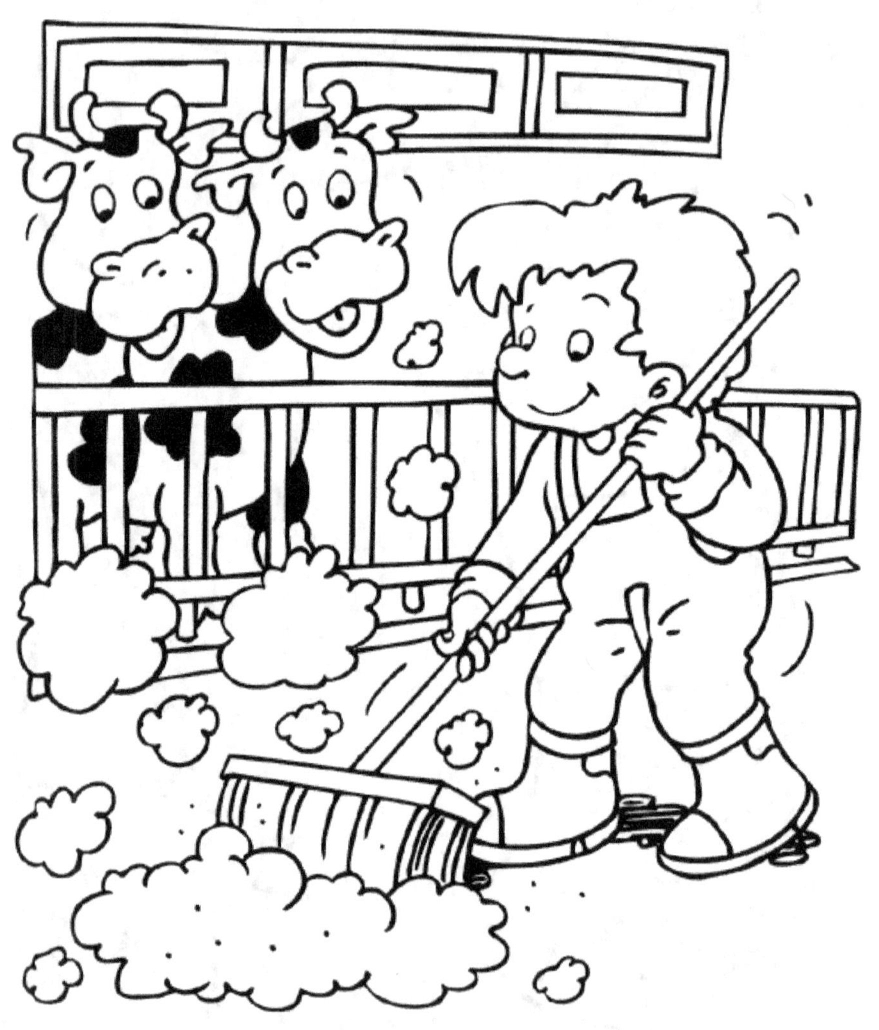

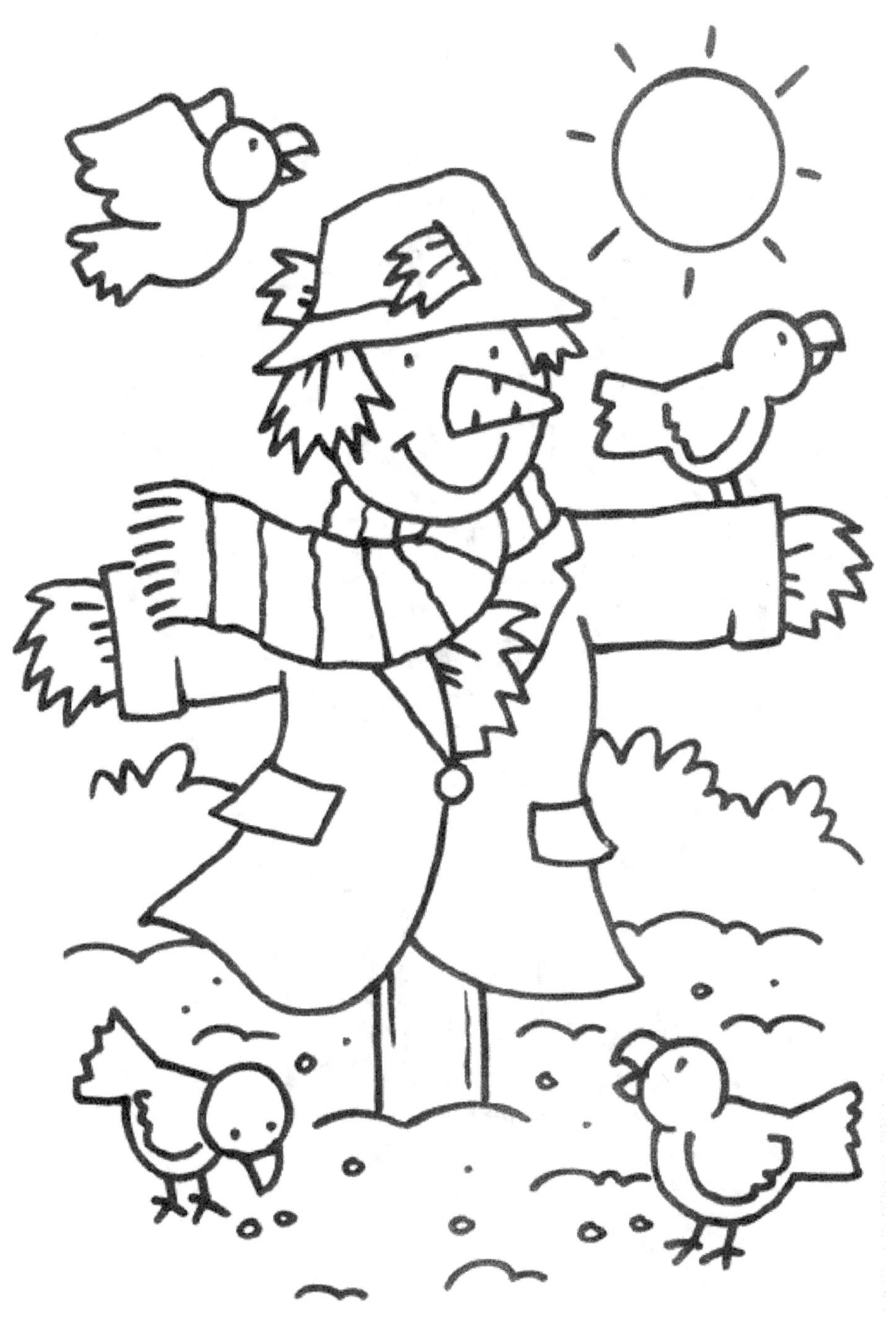

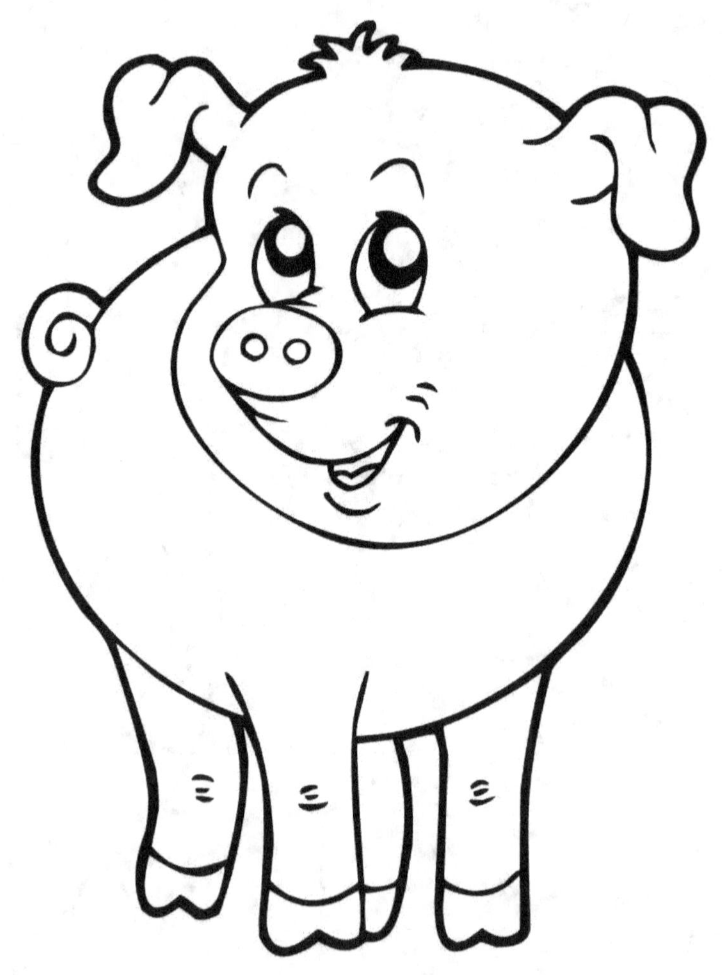

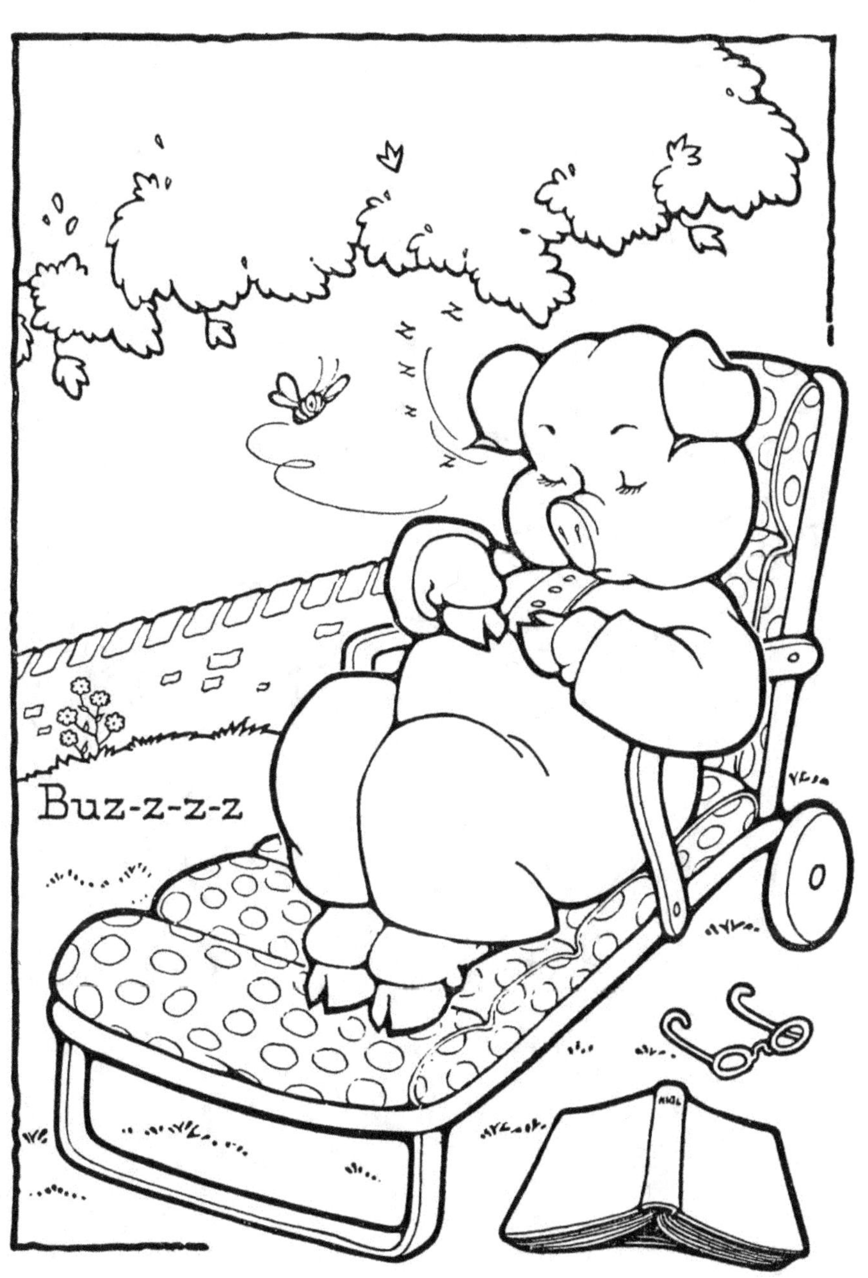

Buz-z-z-z

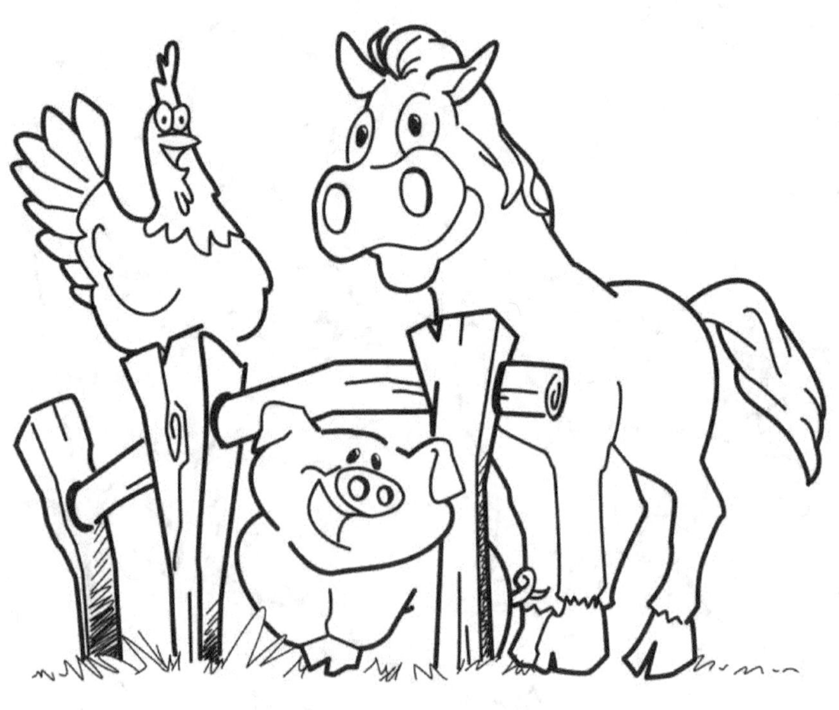

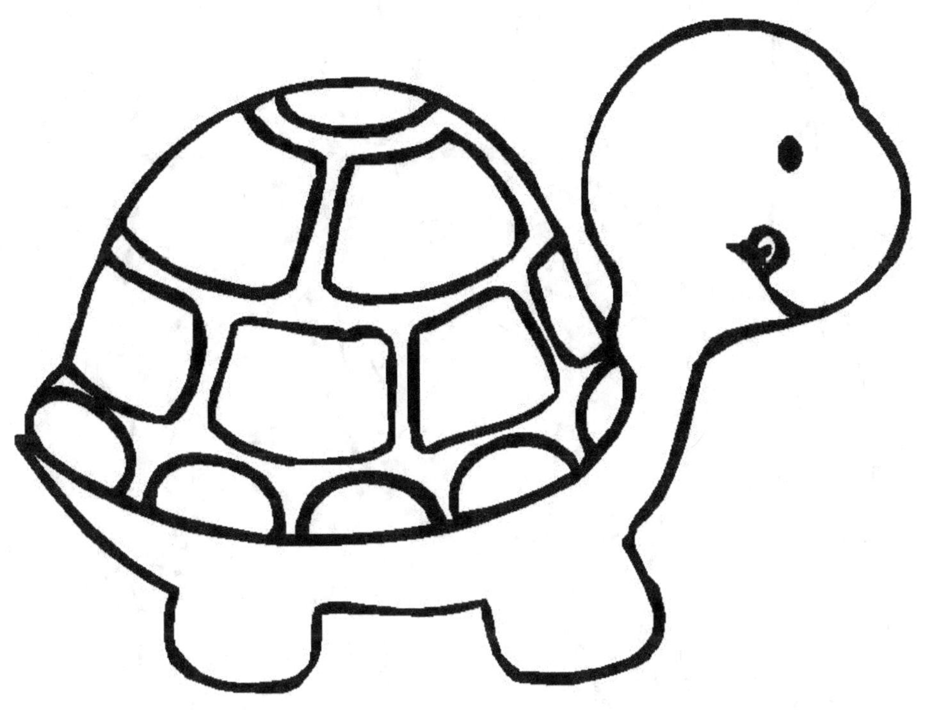

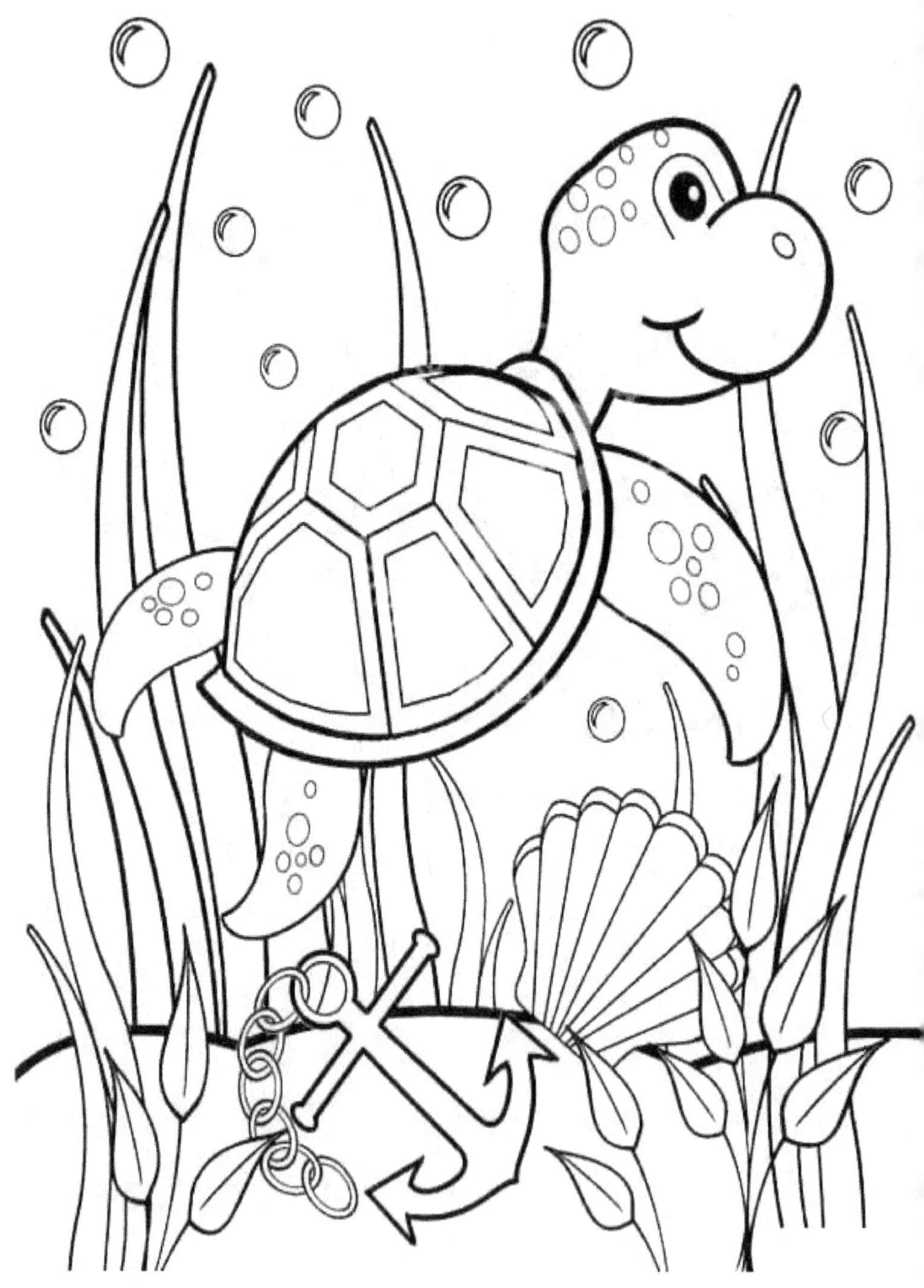

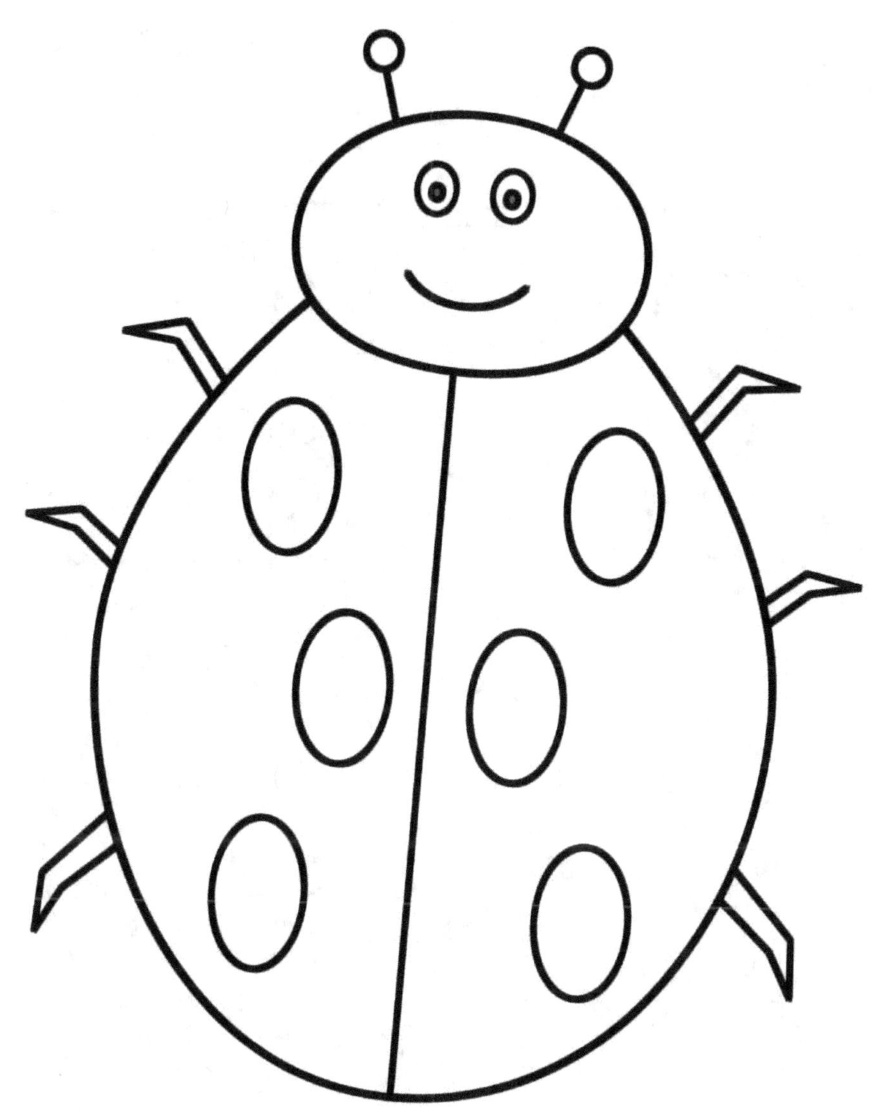

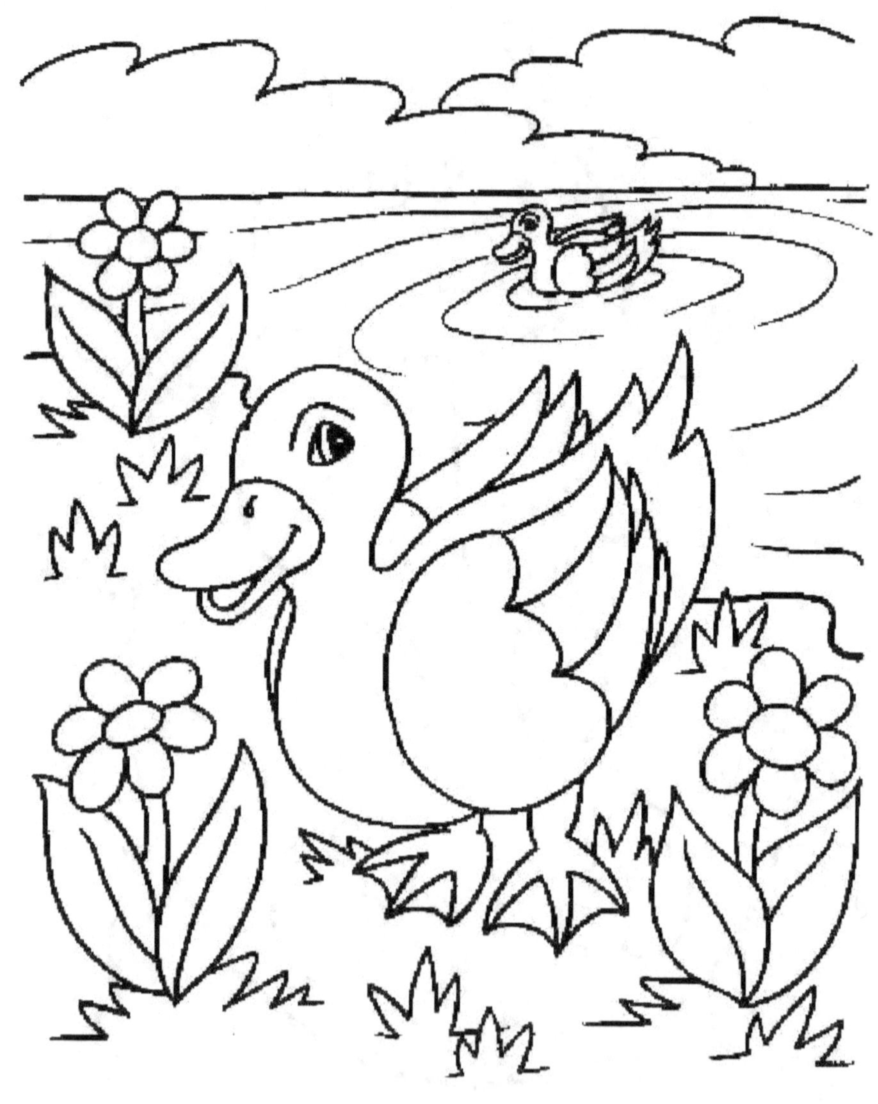

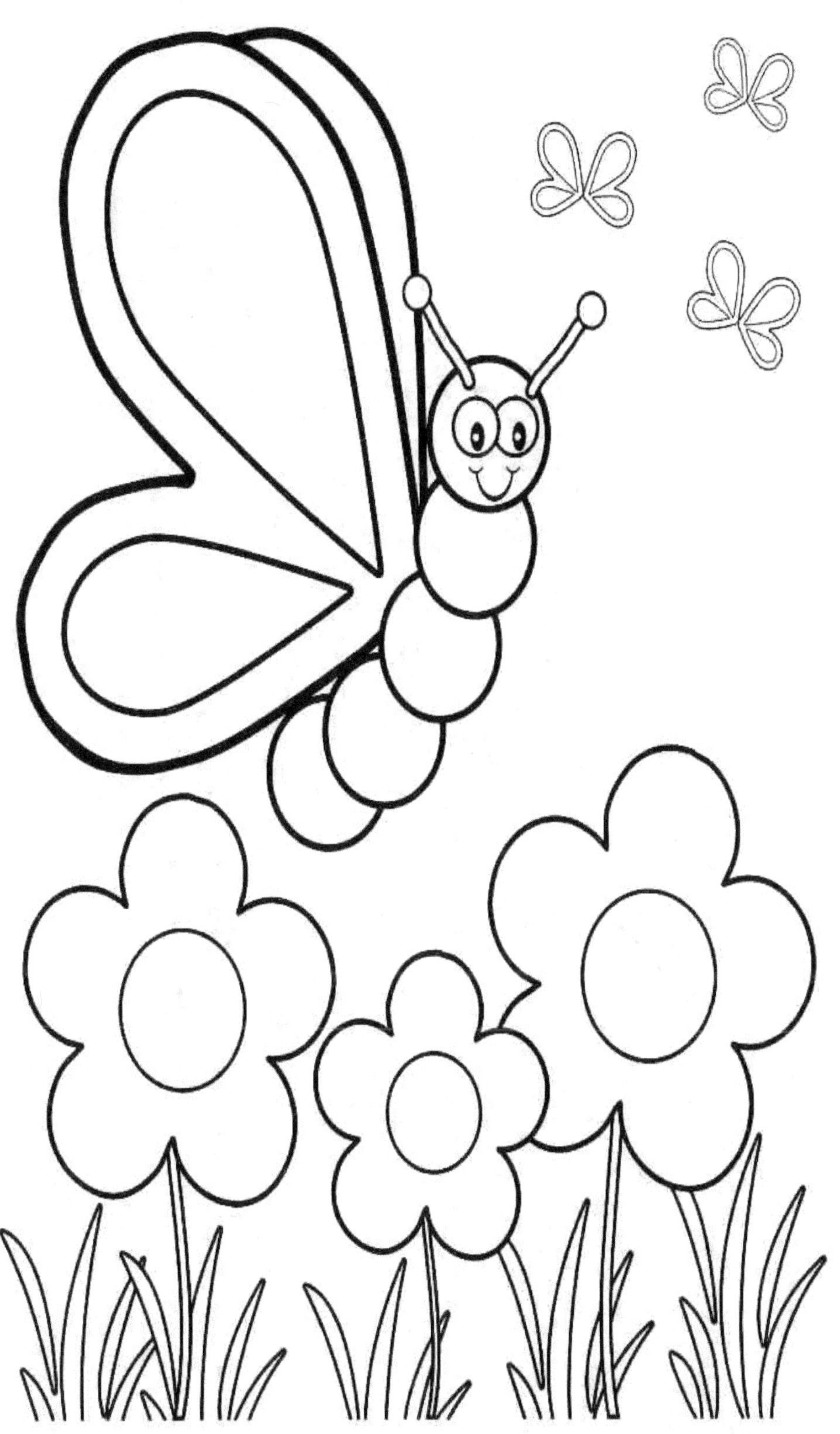

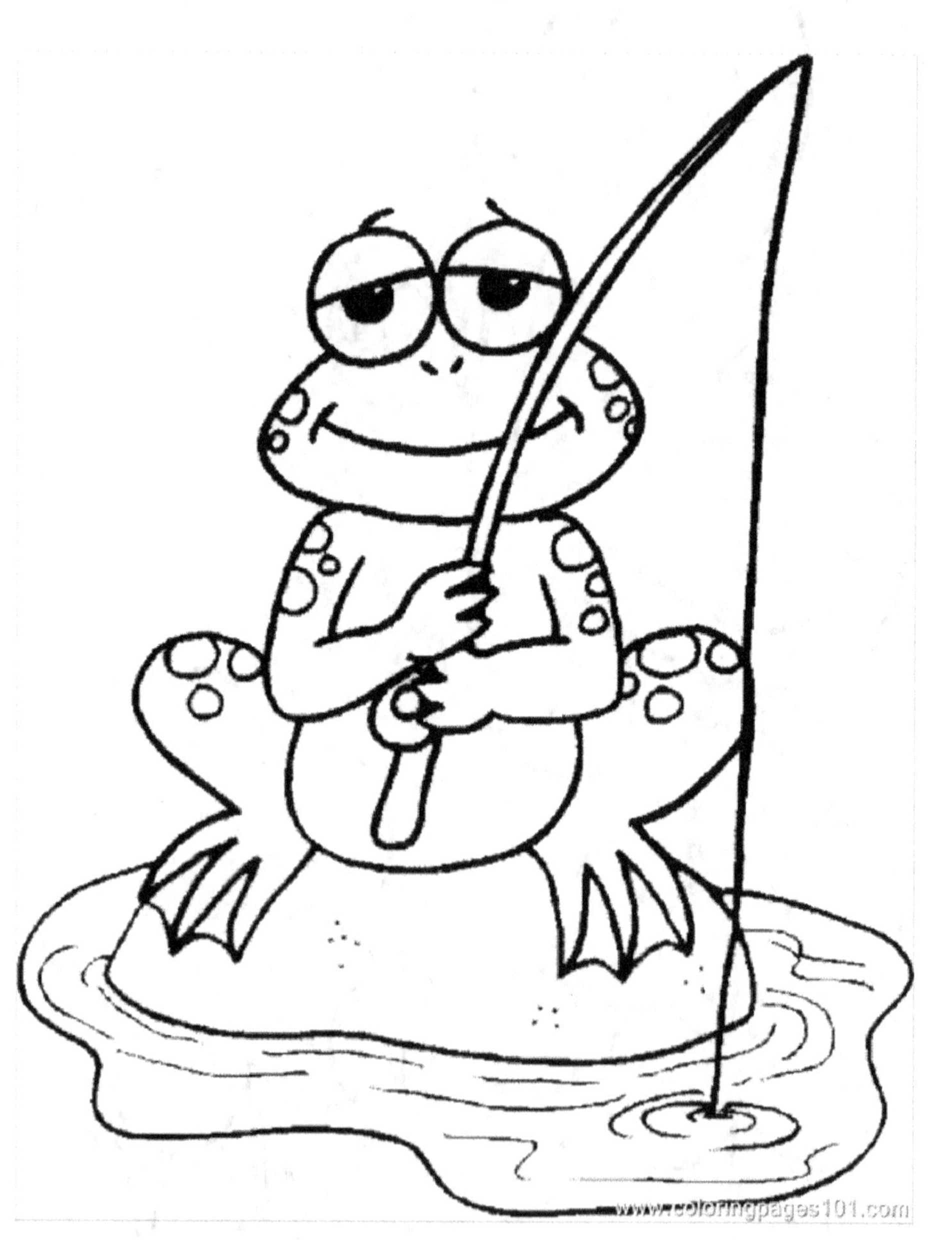
www.coloringpages101.com

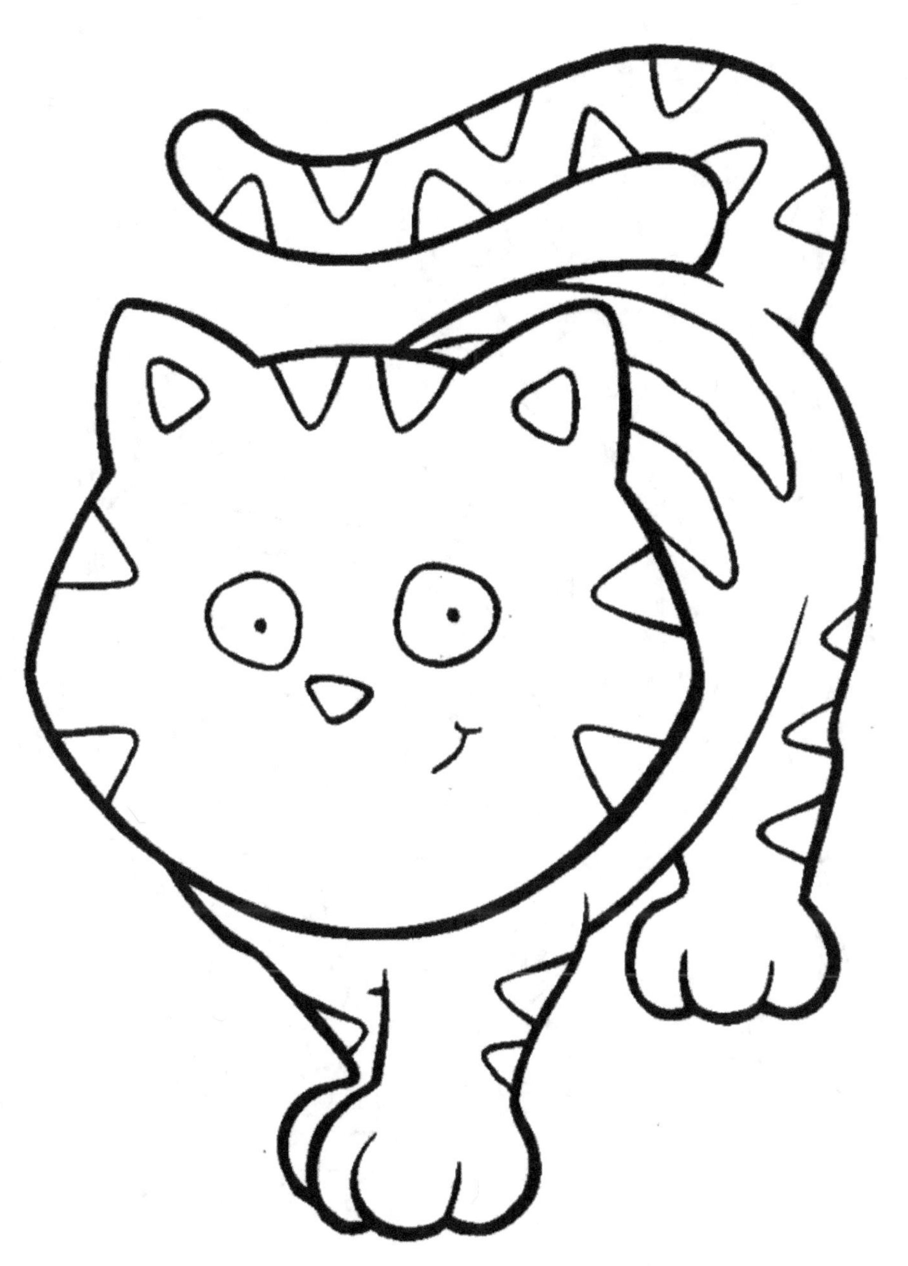

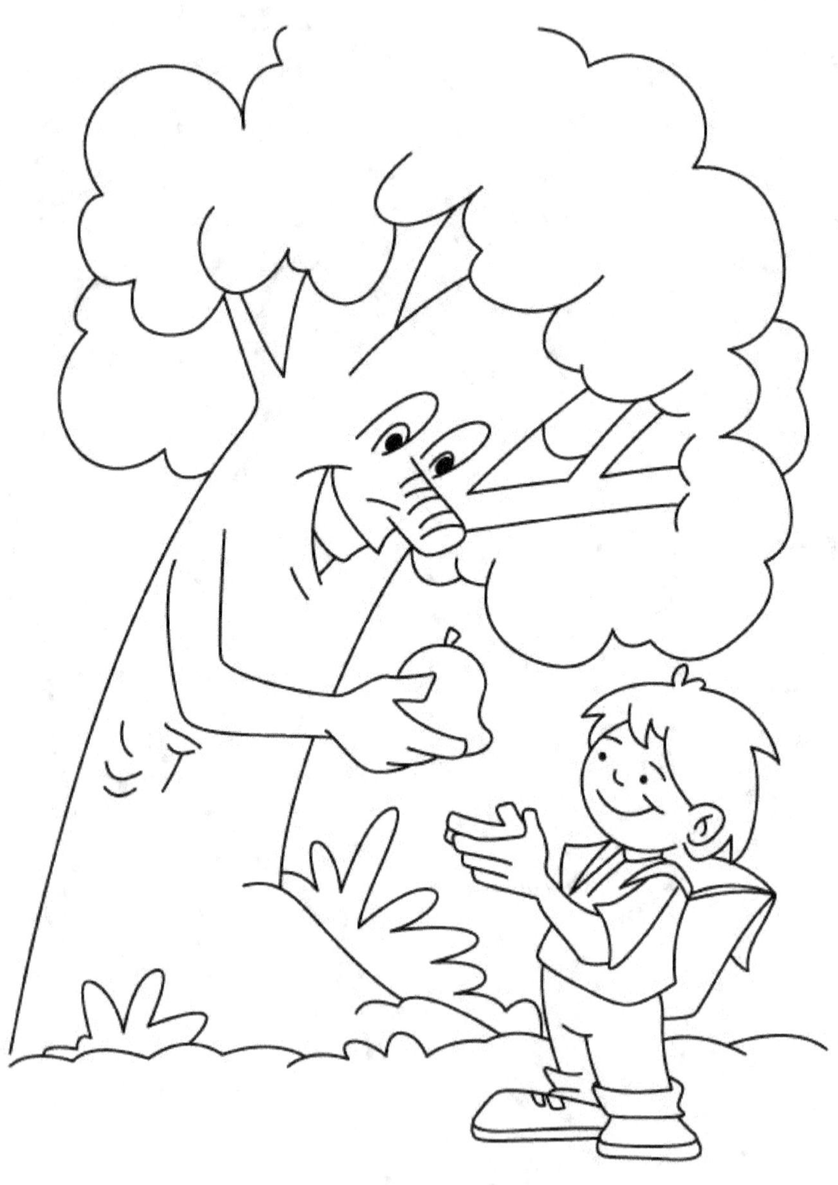

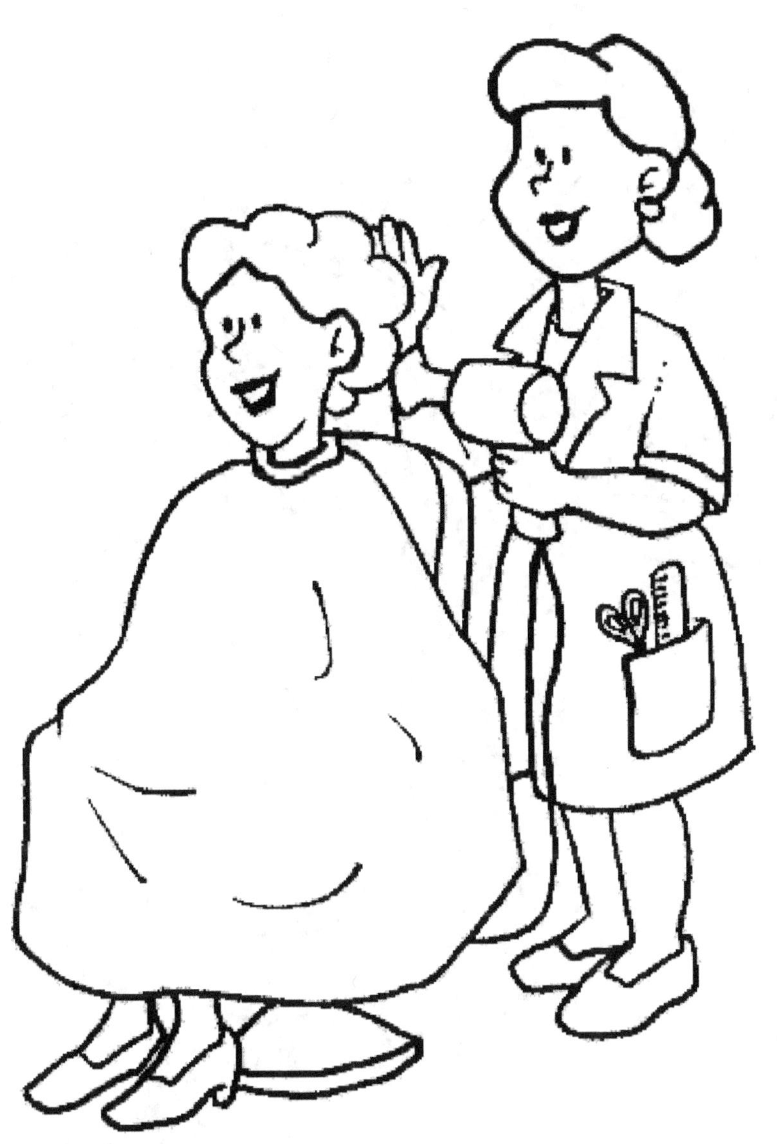

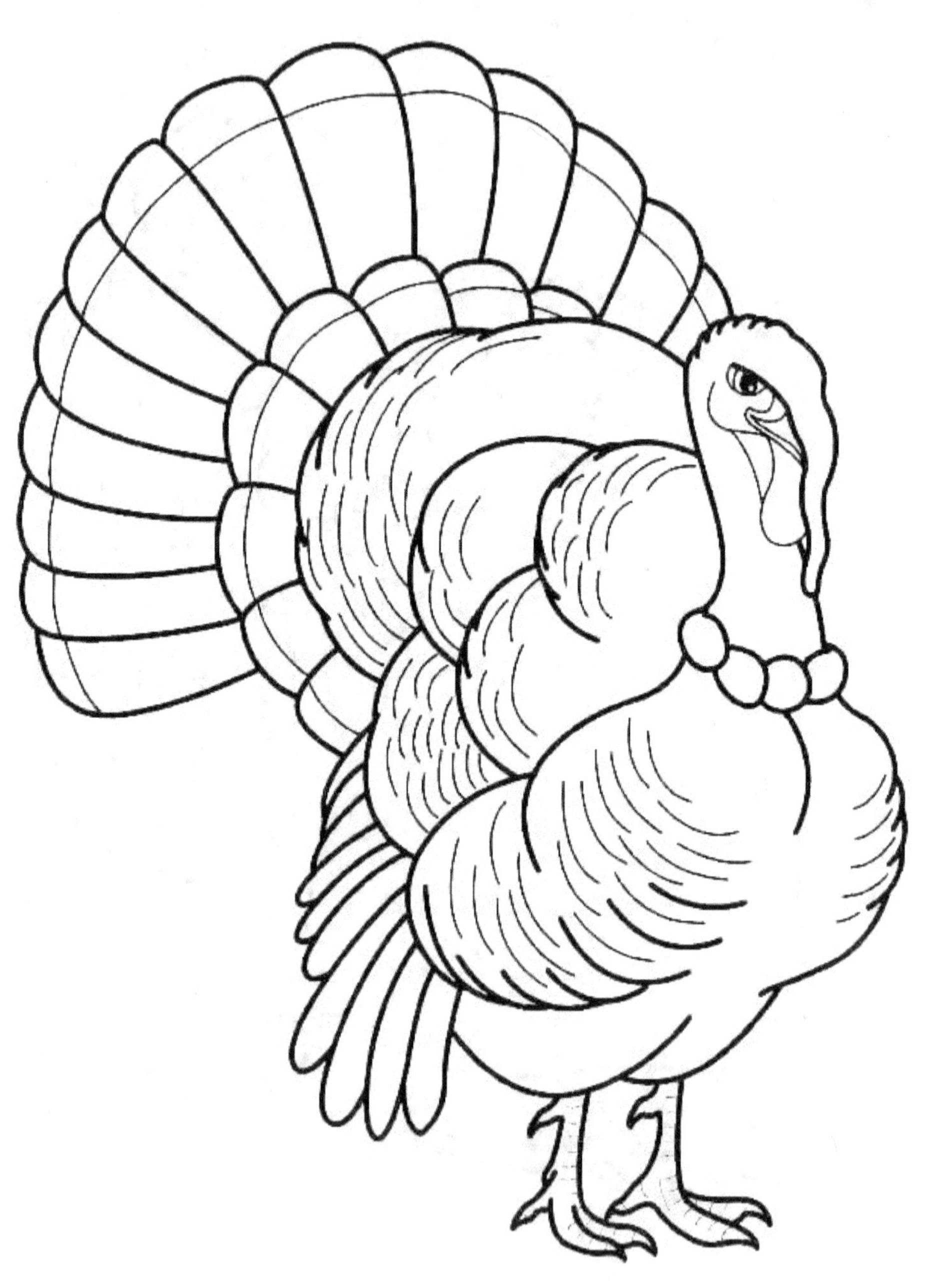

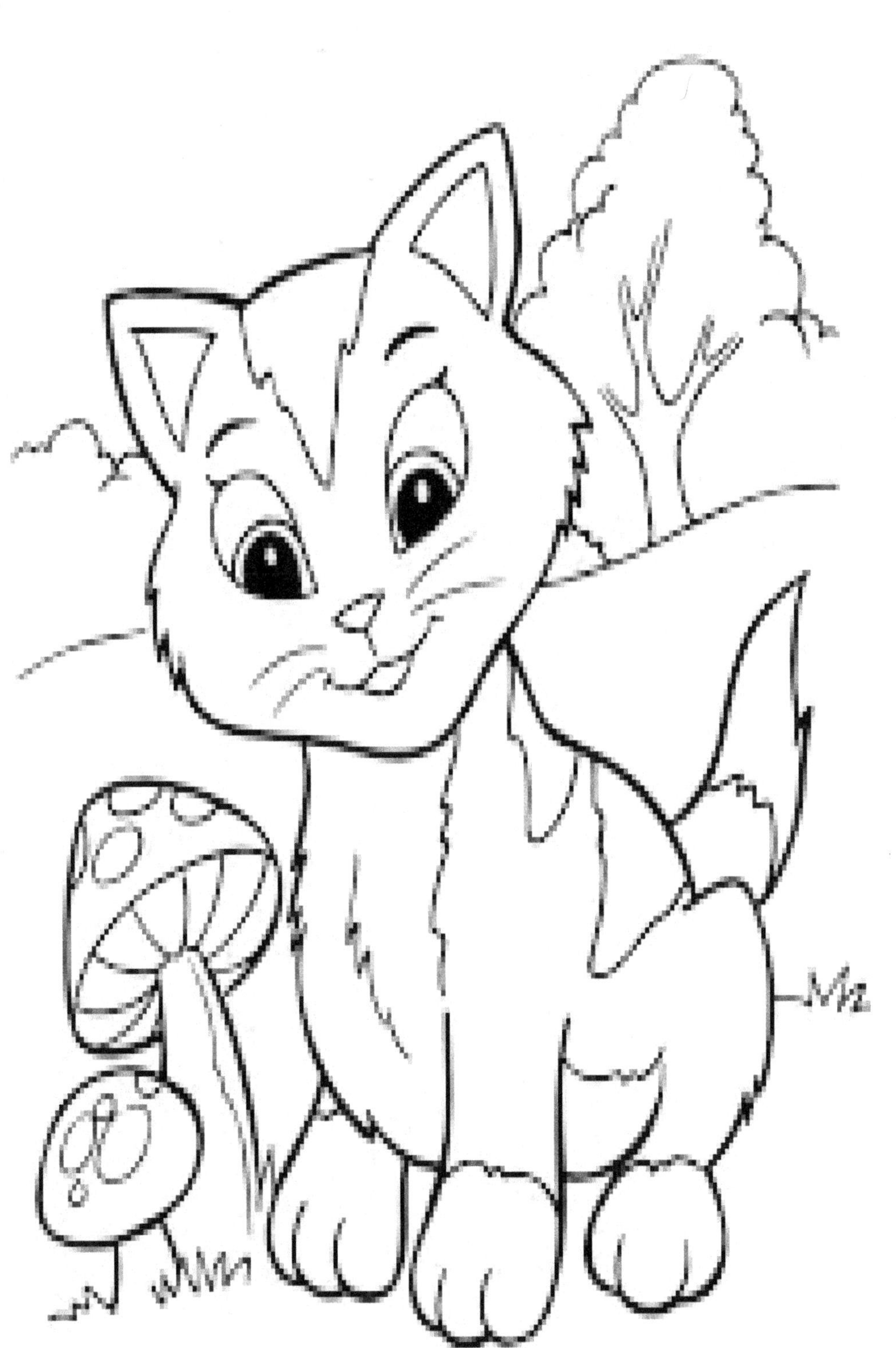

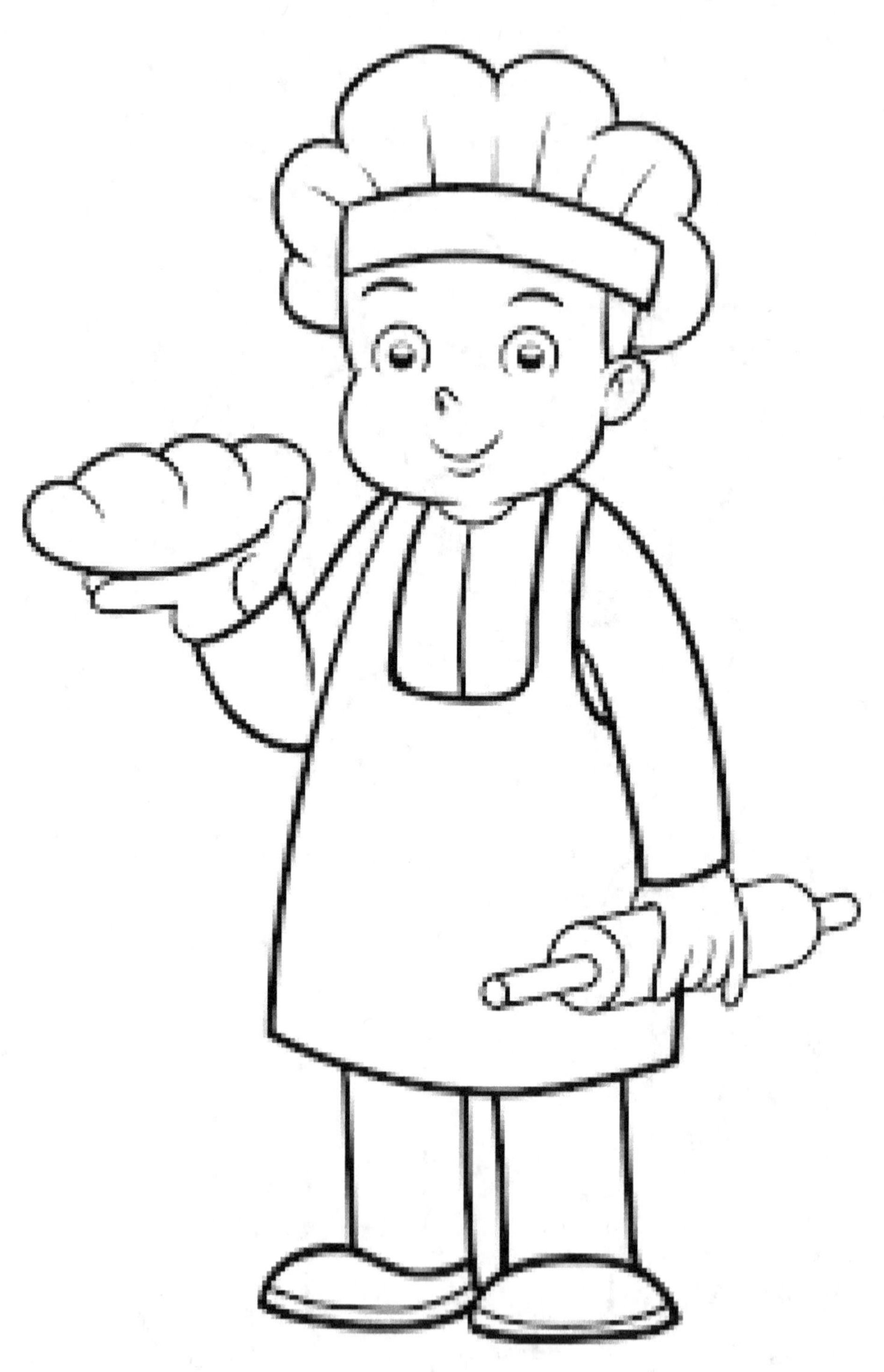

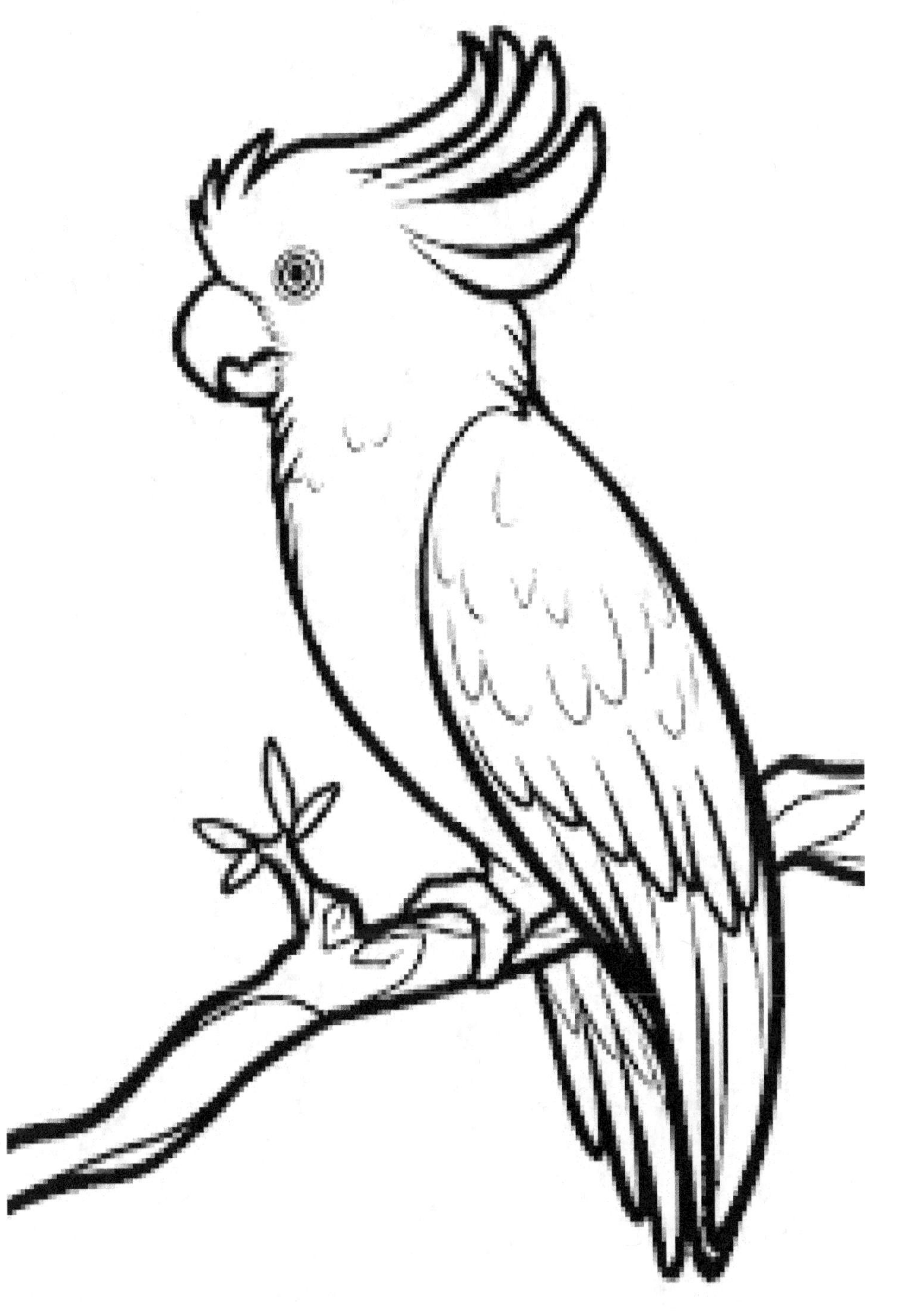

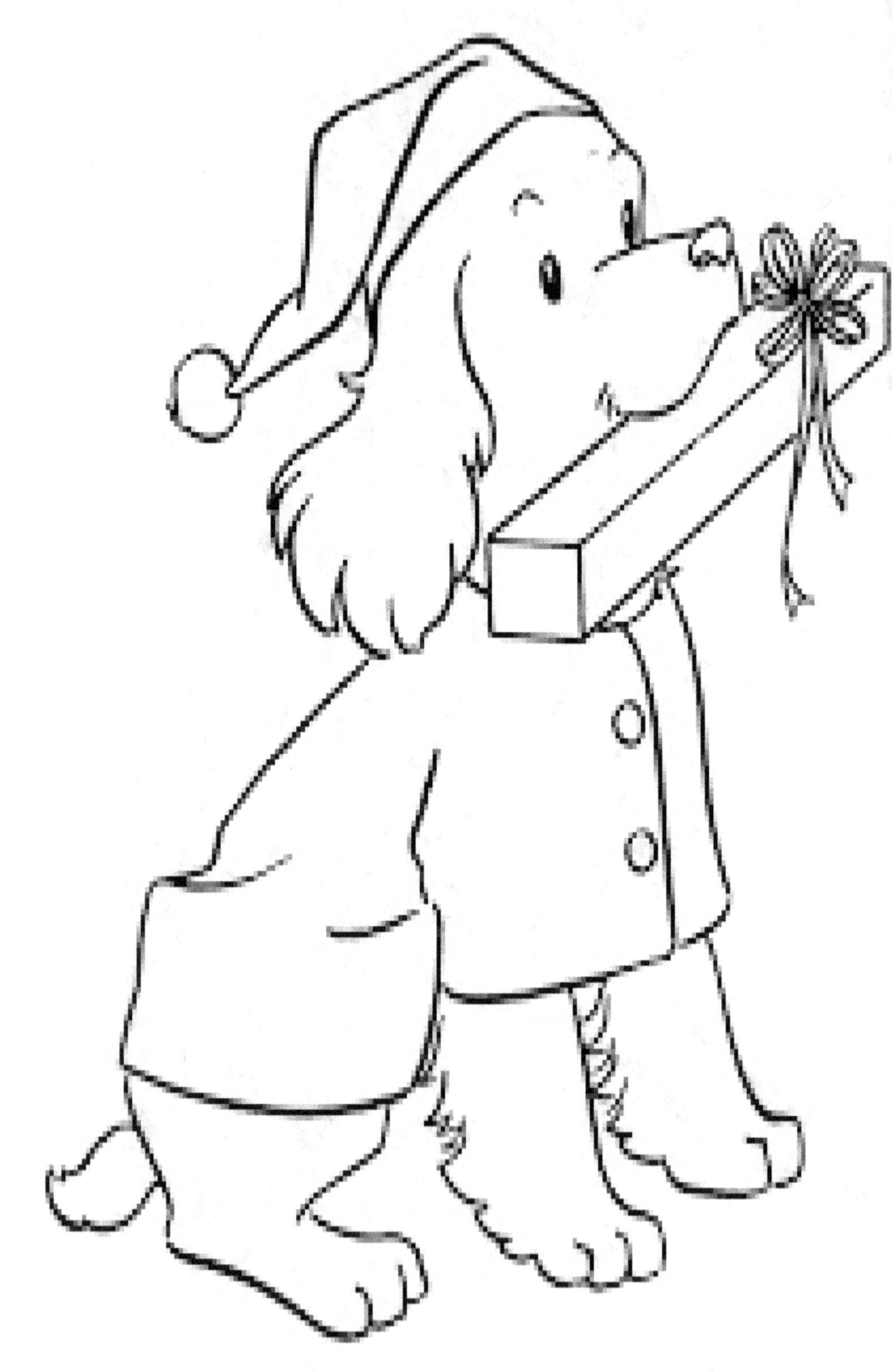

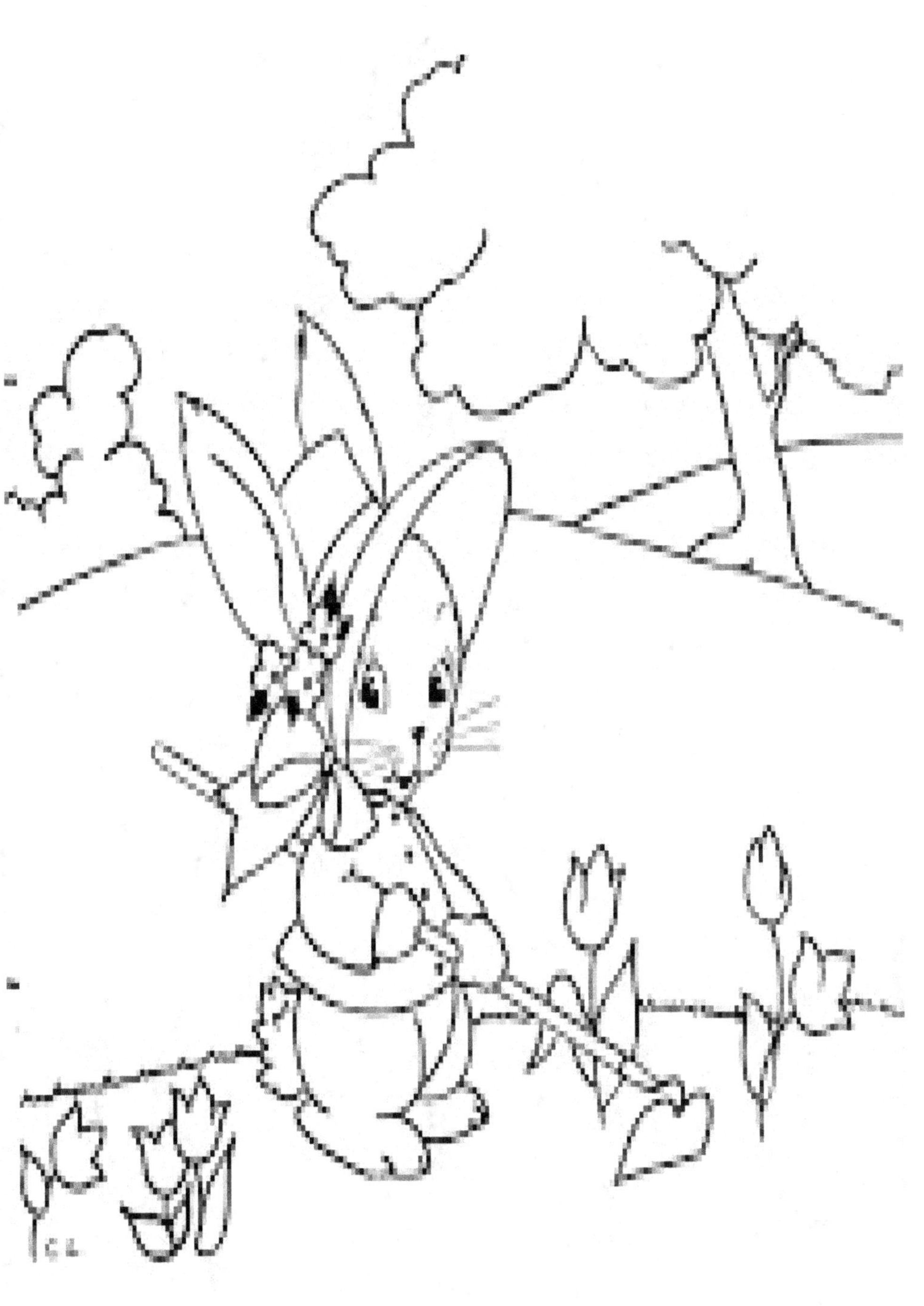

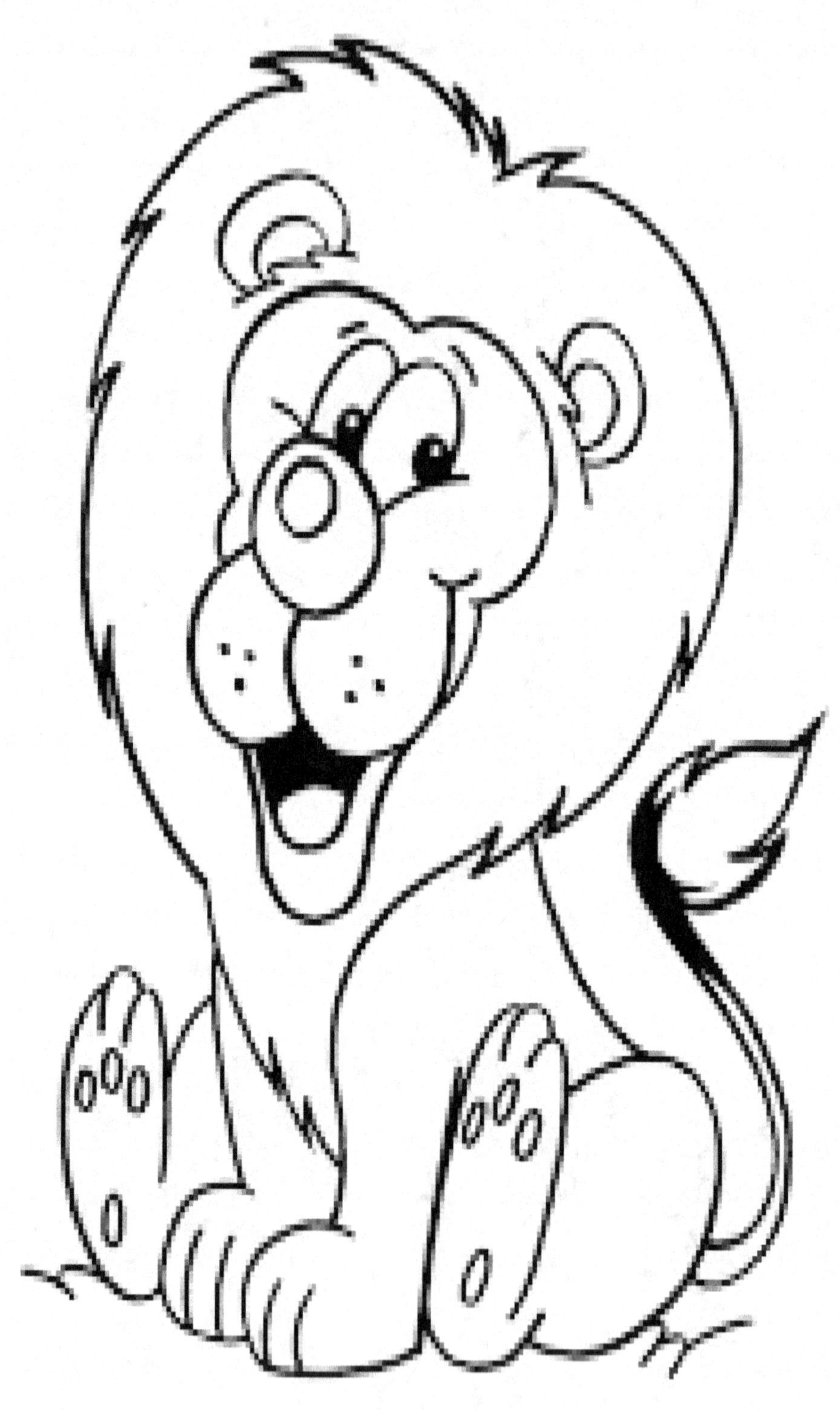

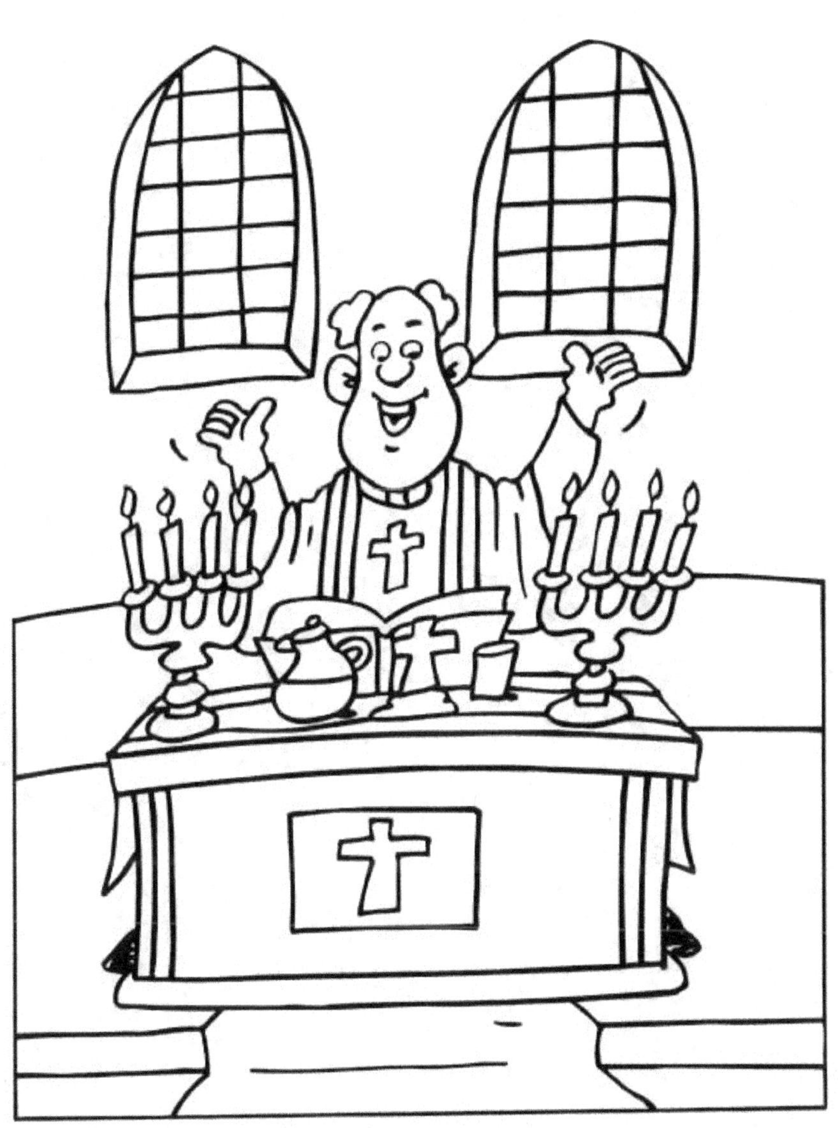

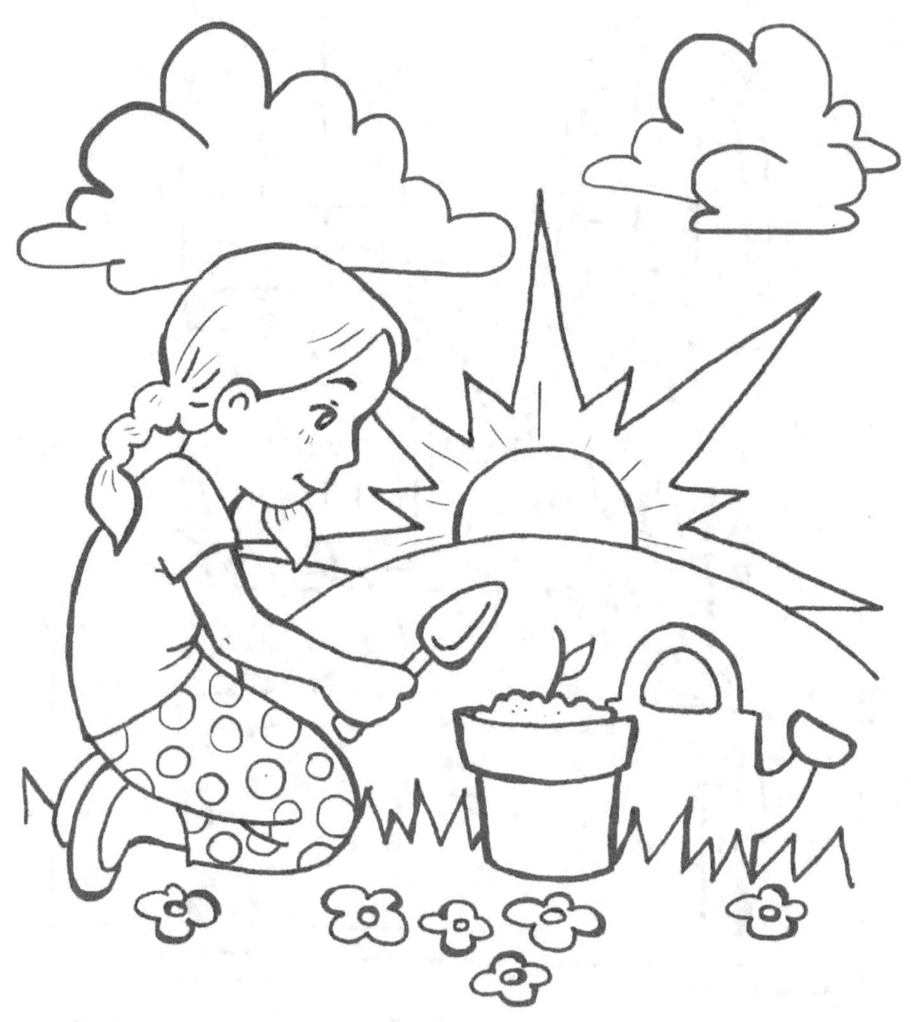

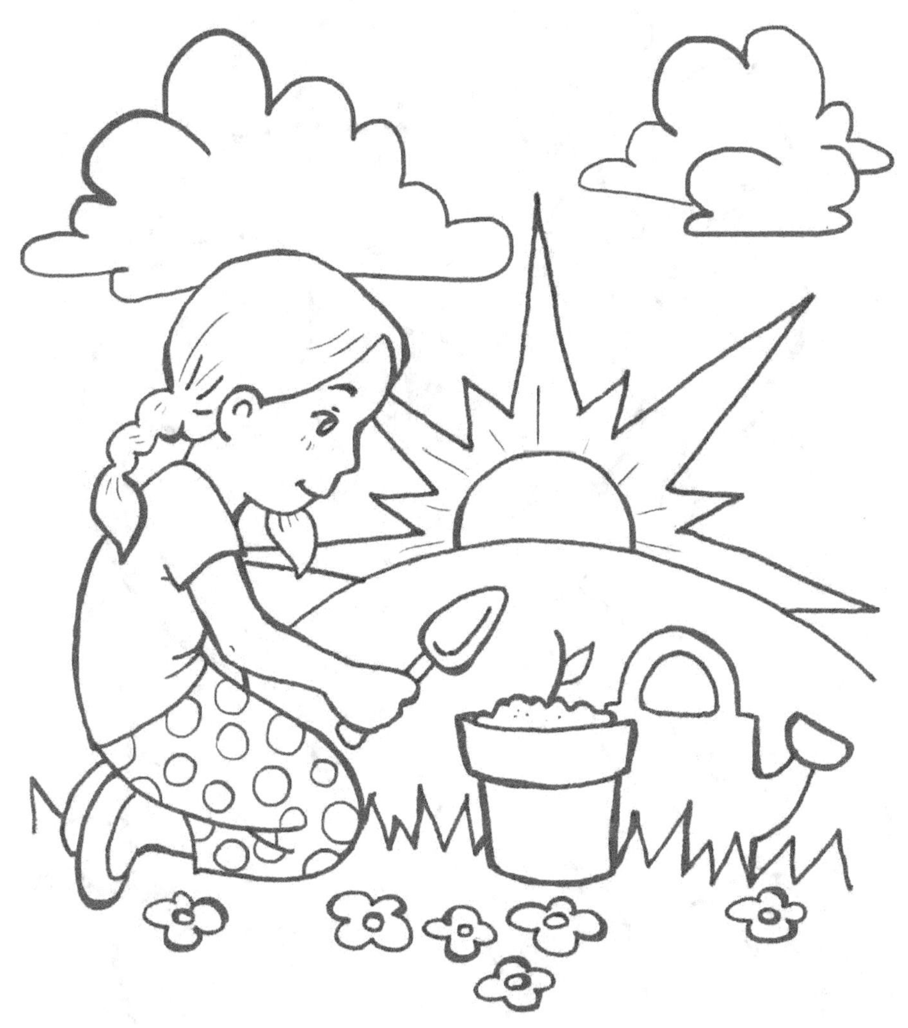

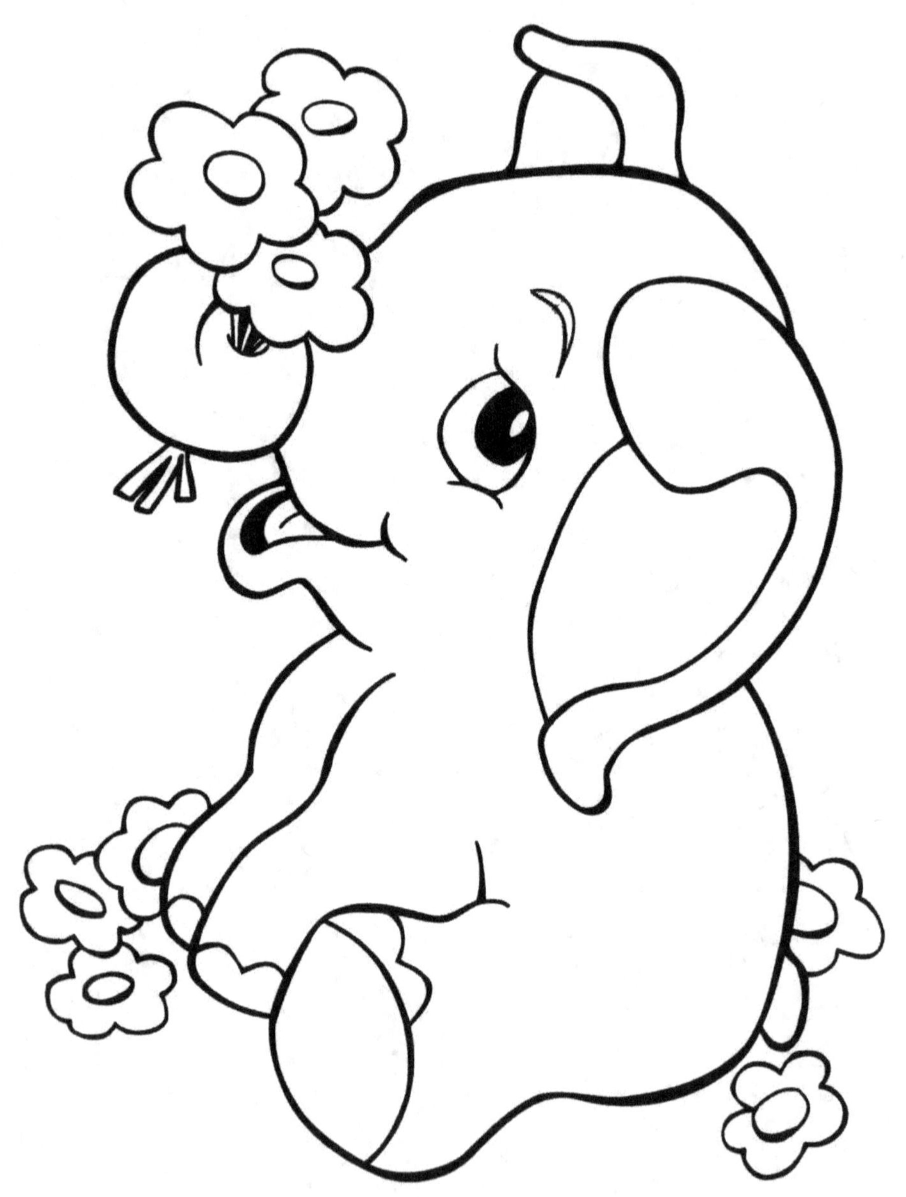

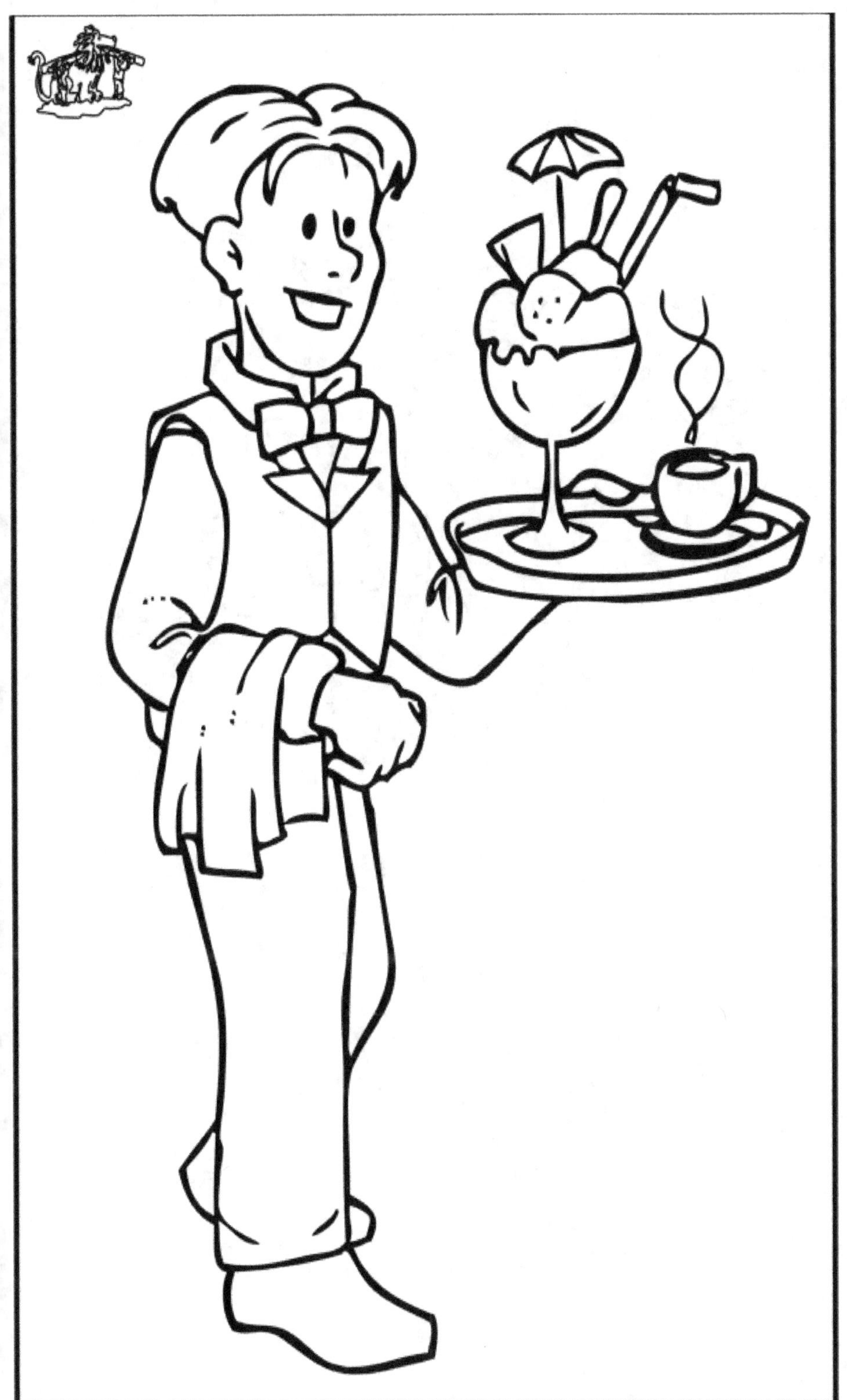

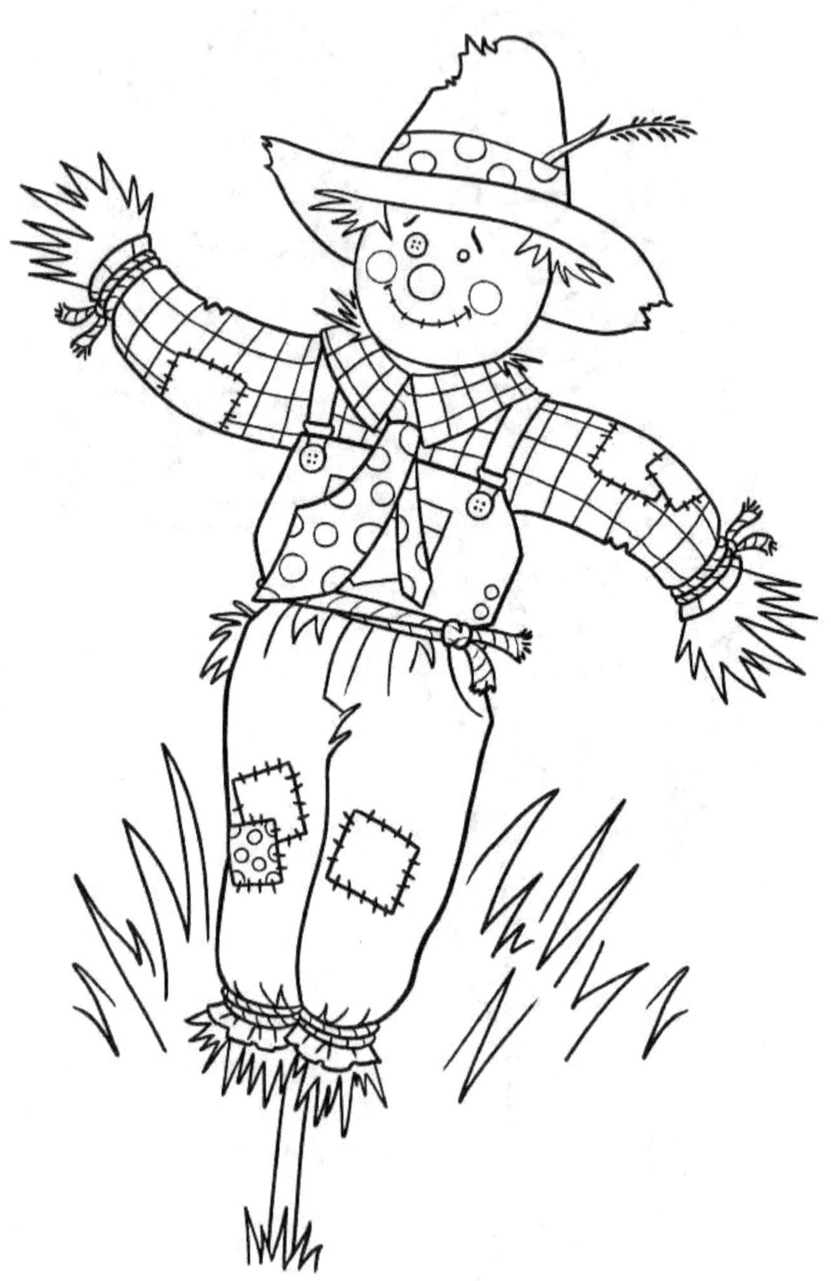

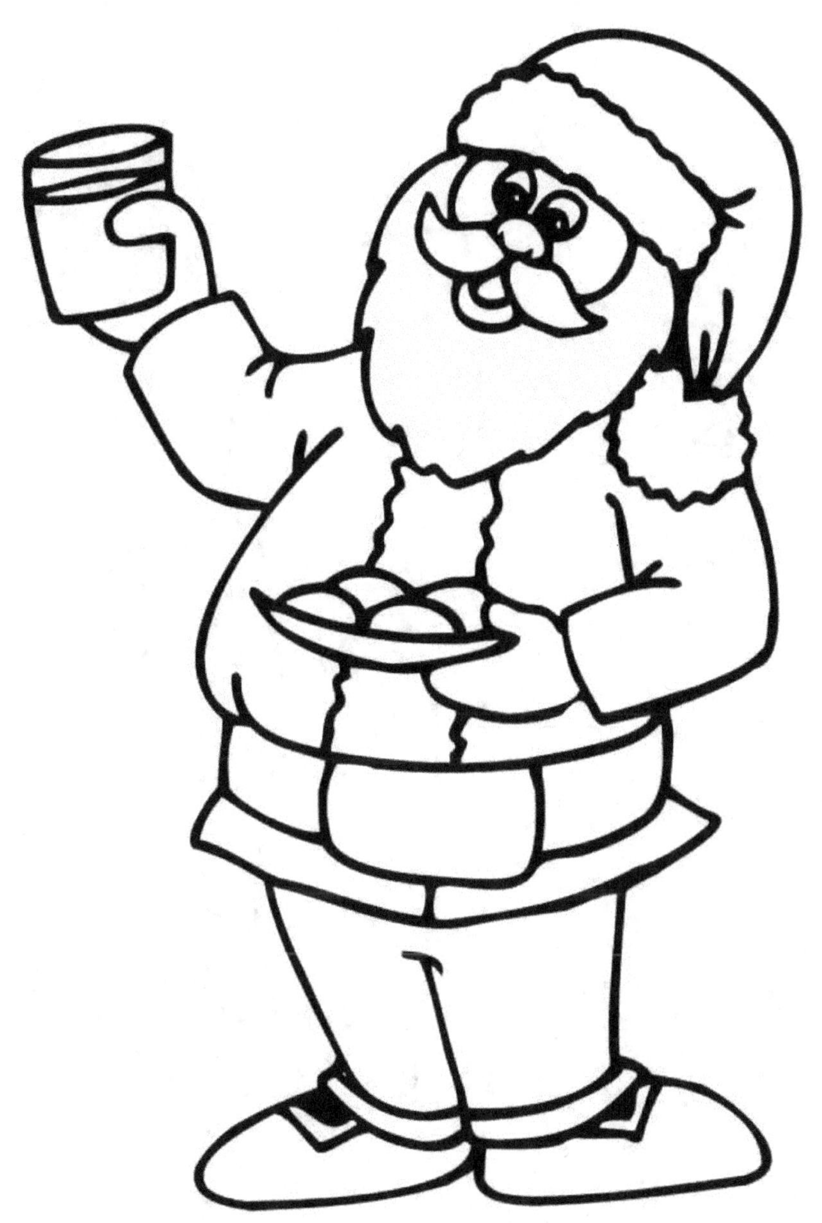

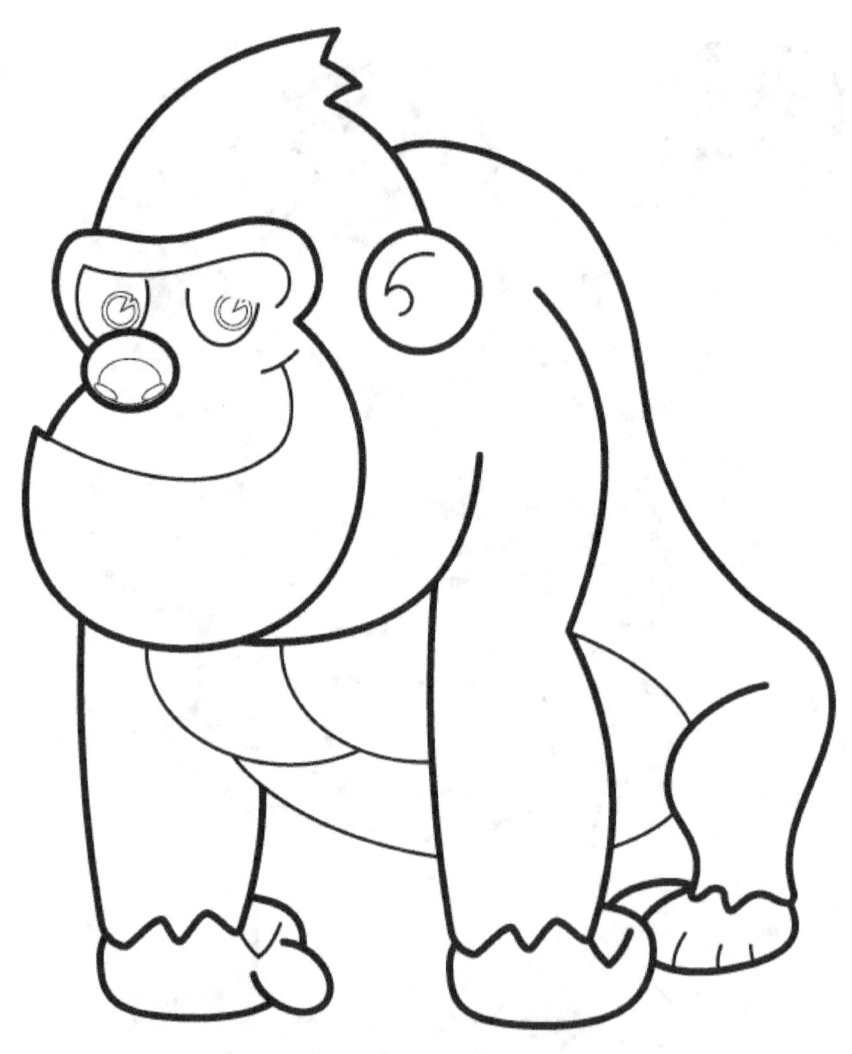

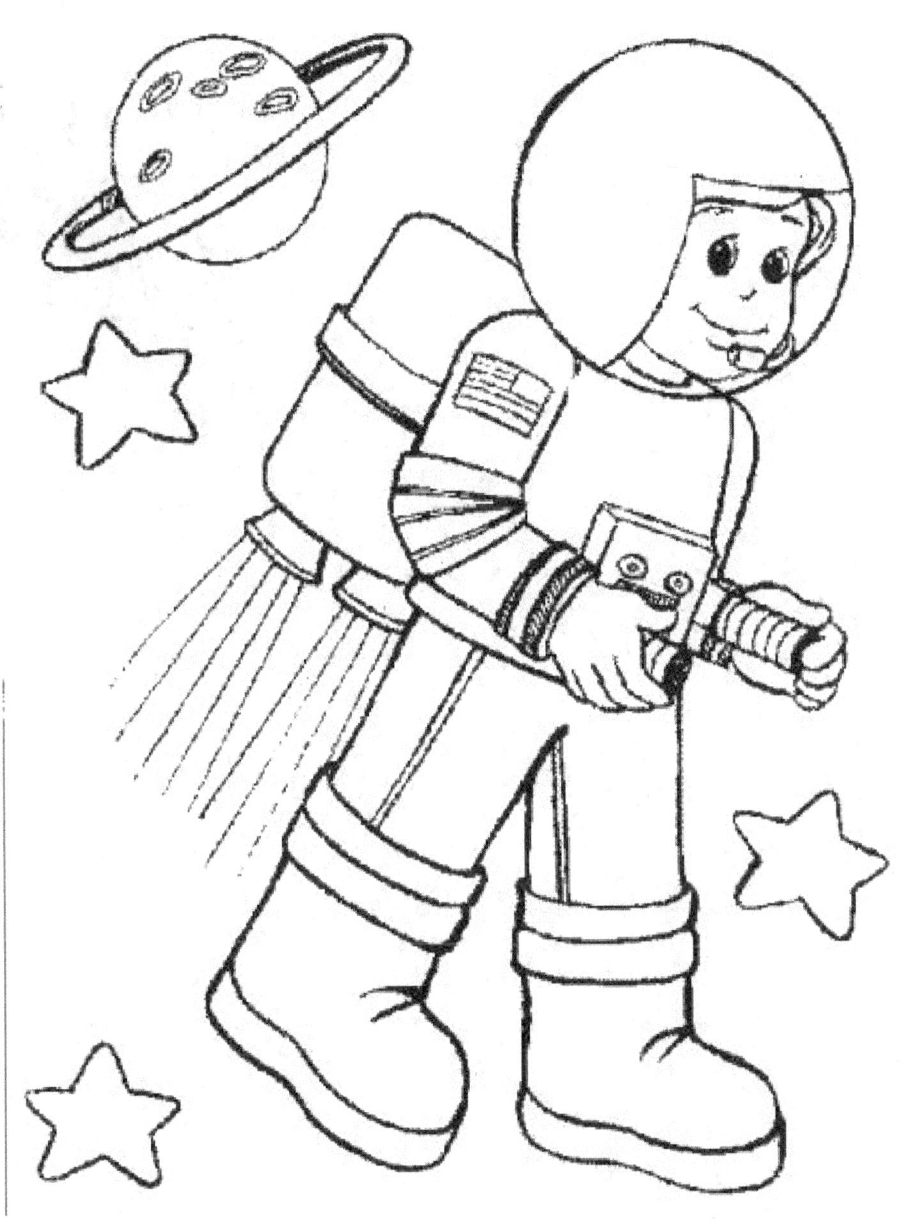

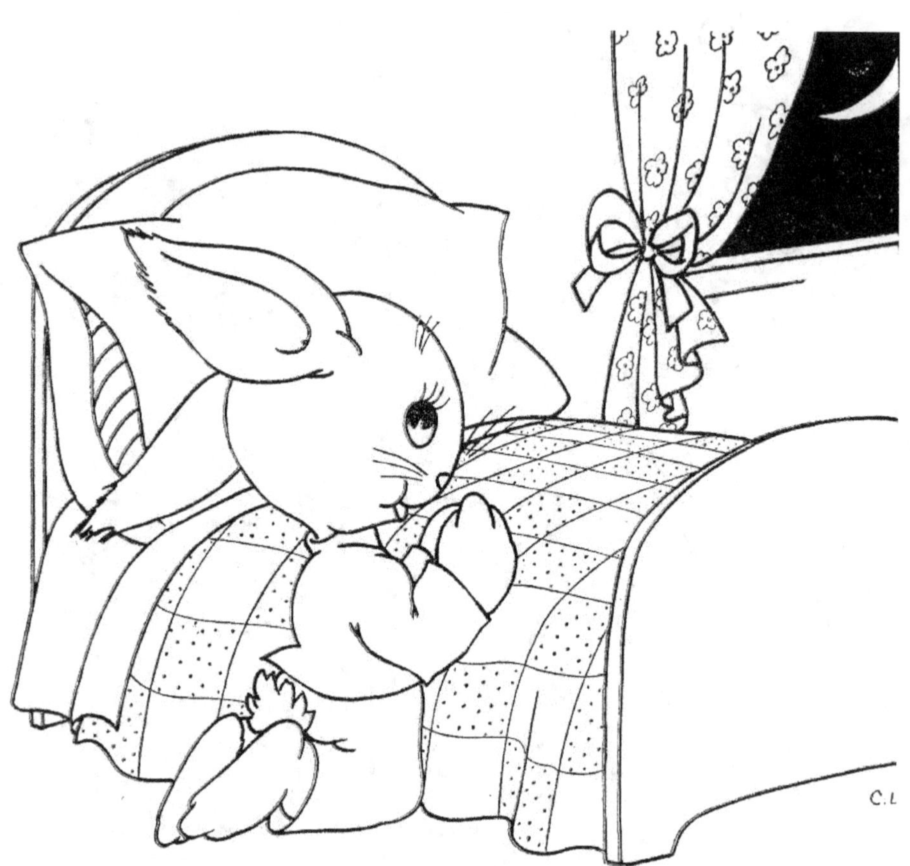

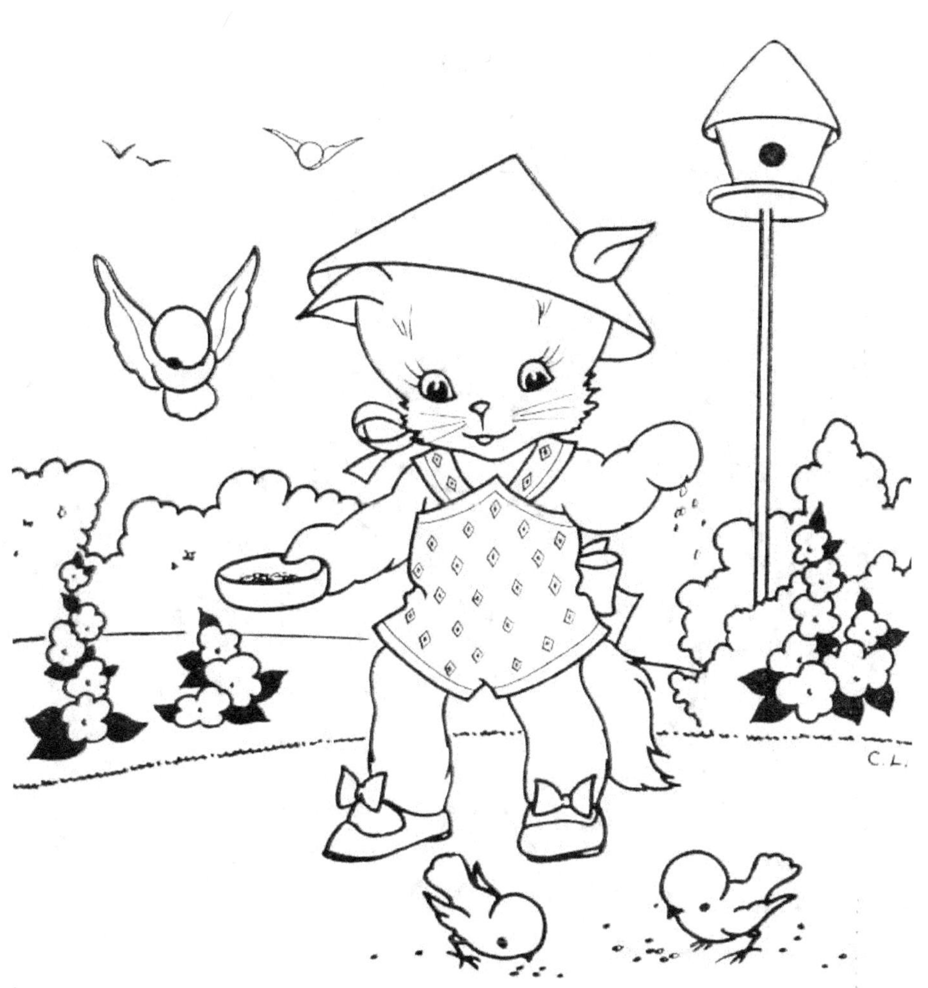

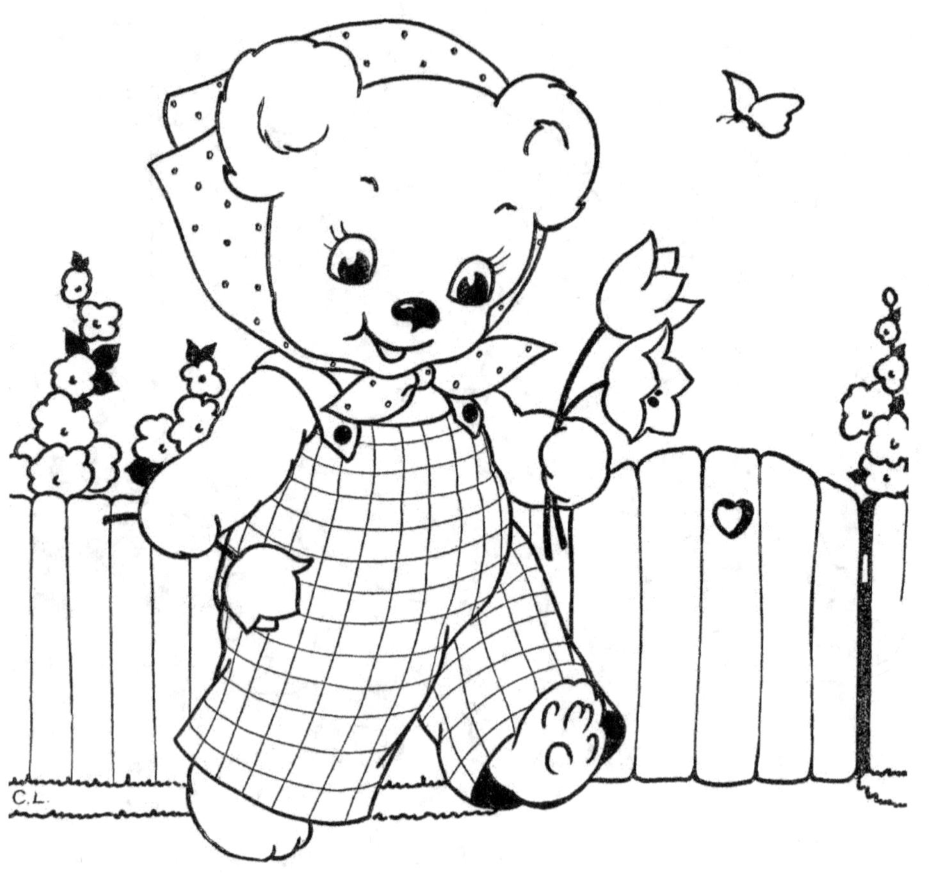

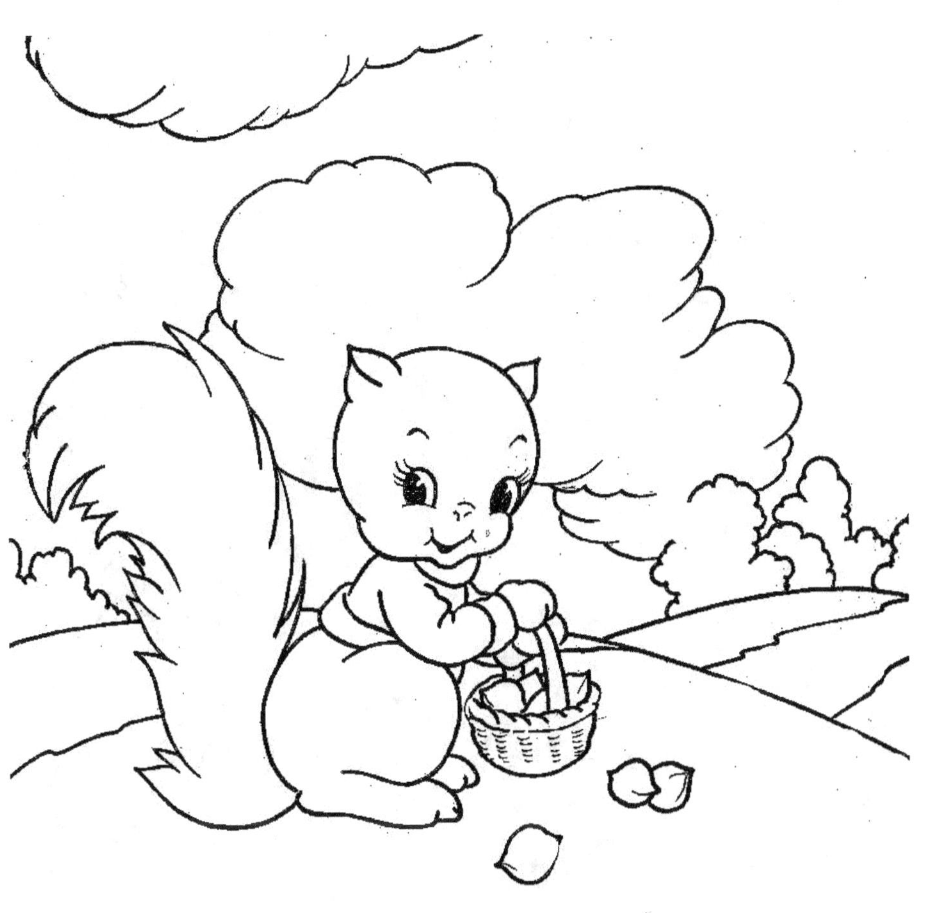

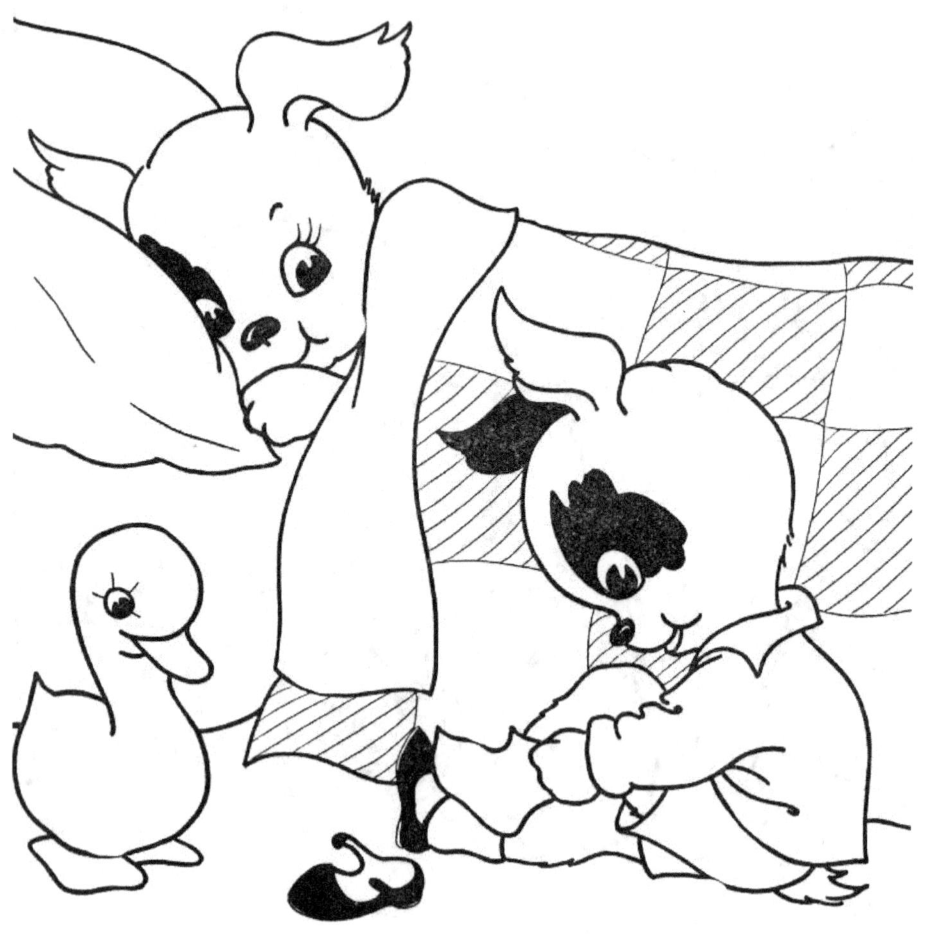

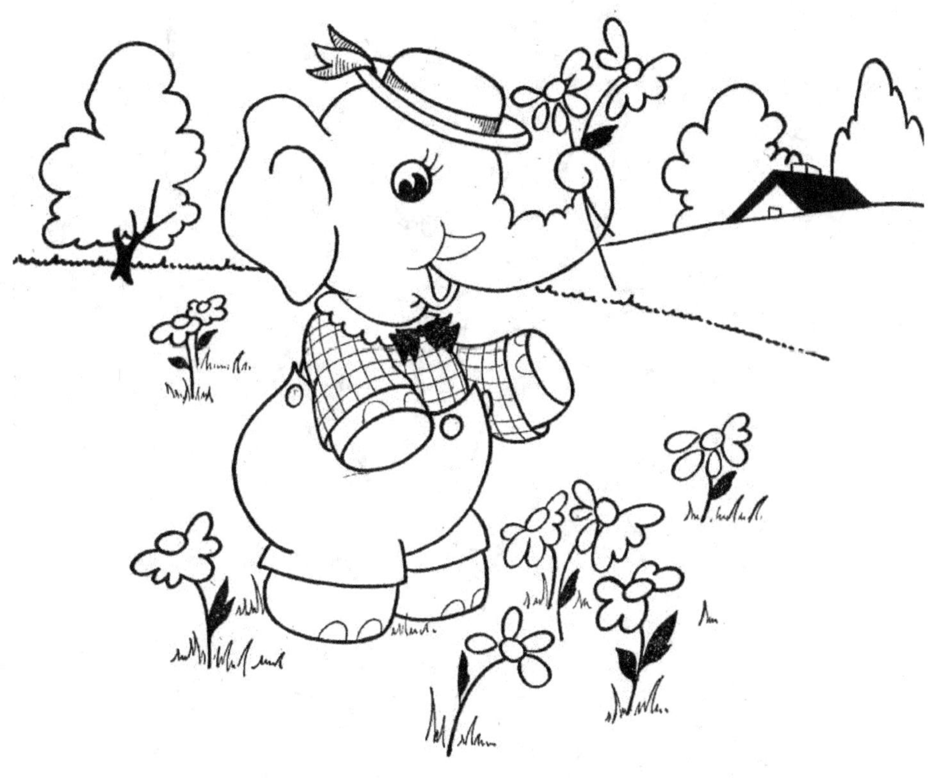

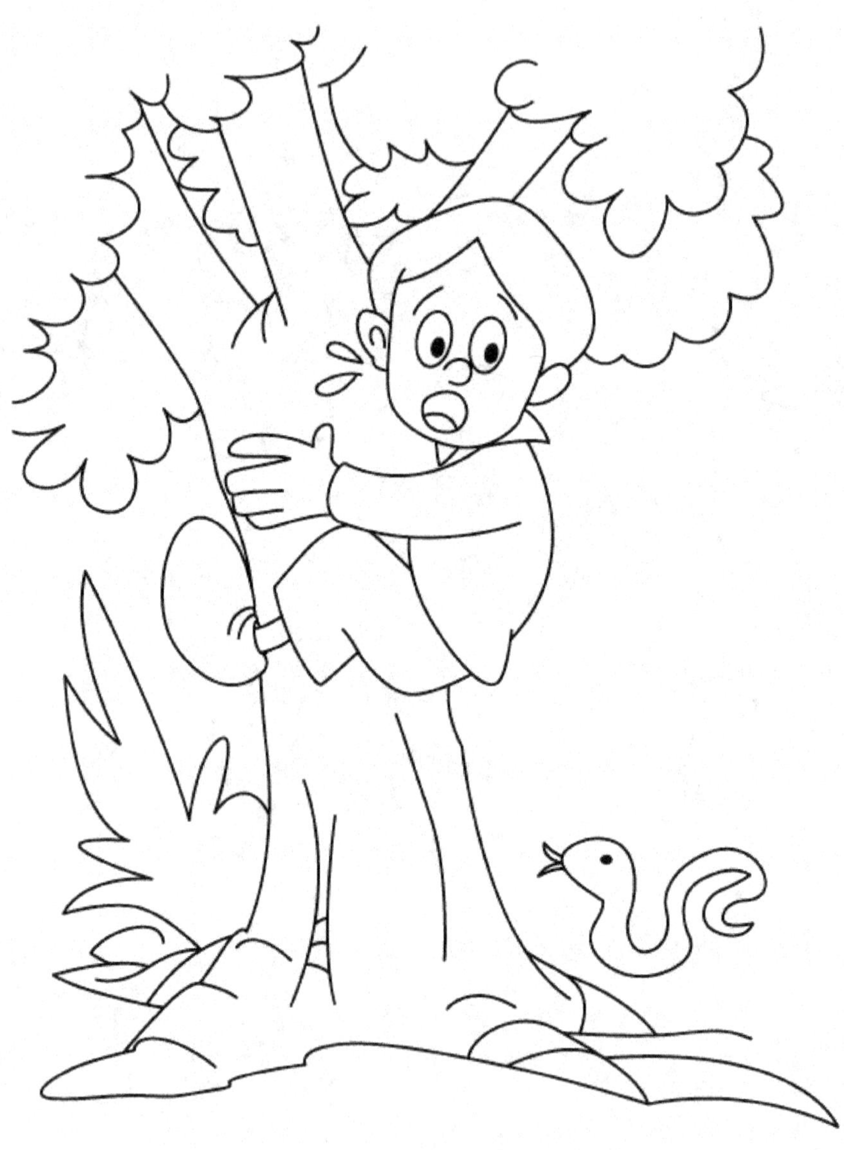

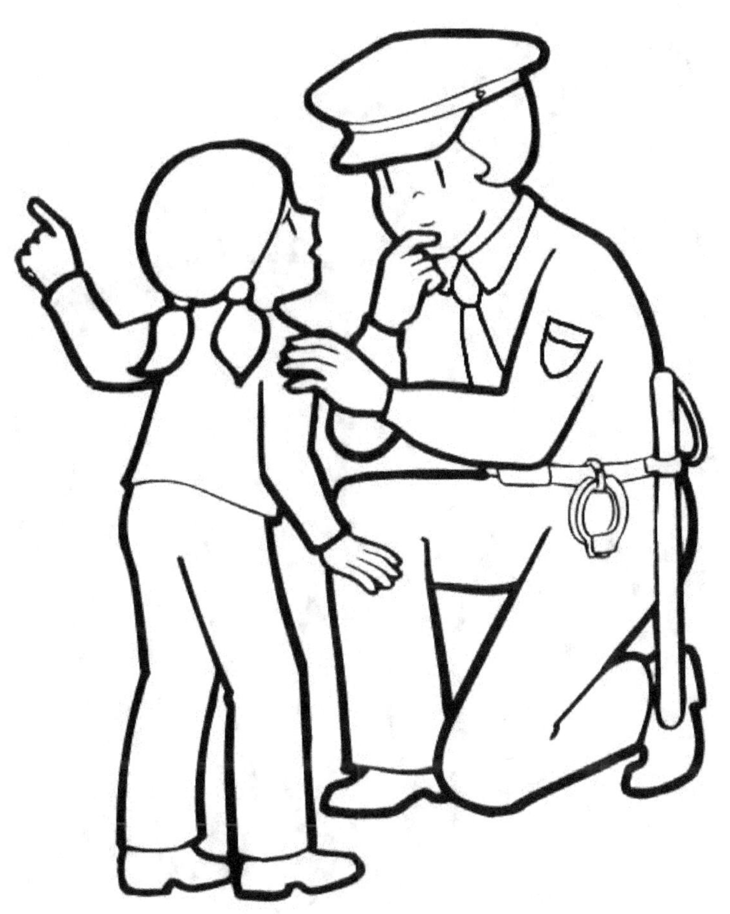

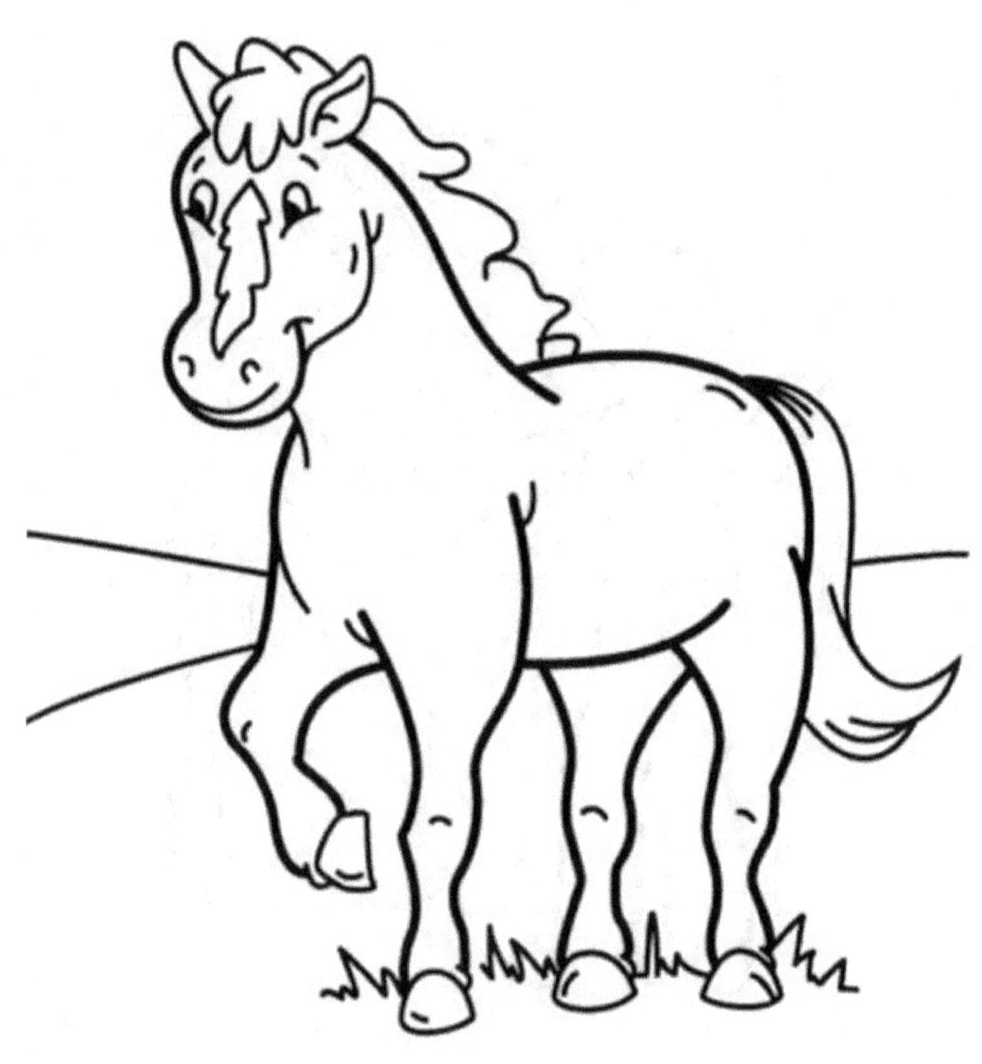

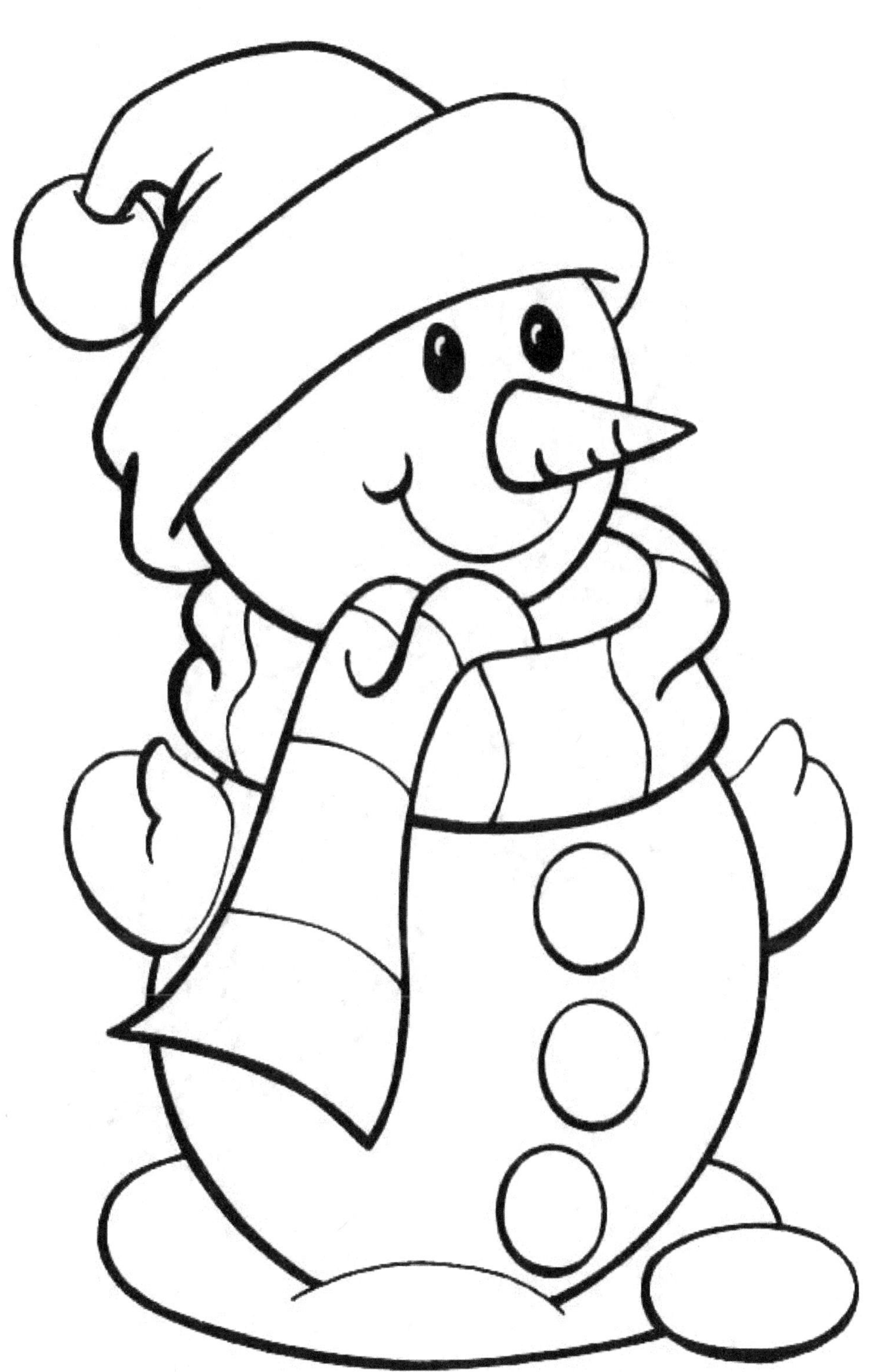

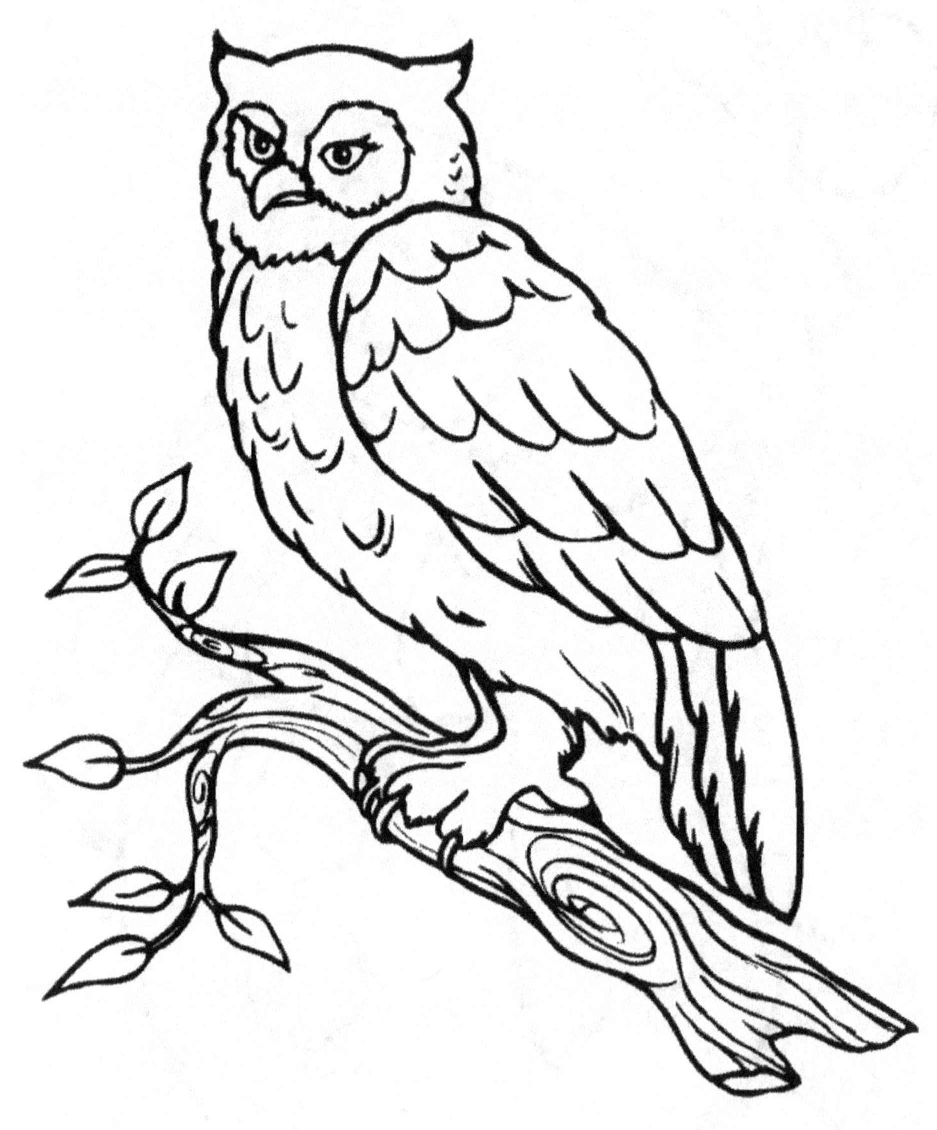

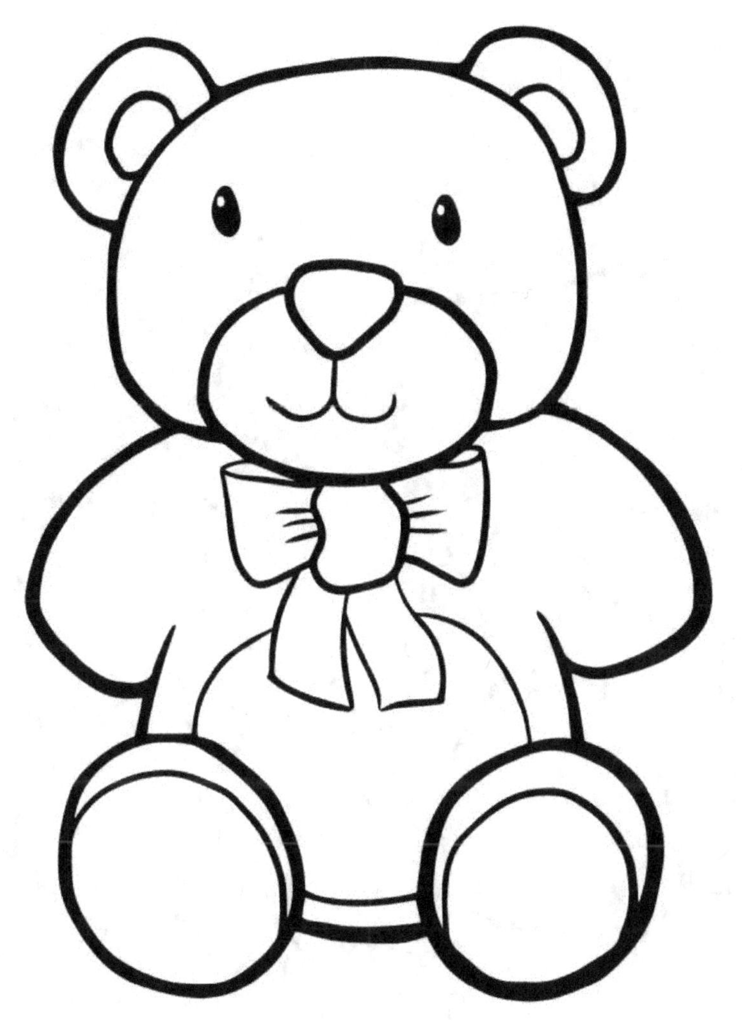

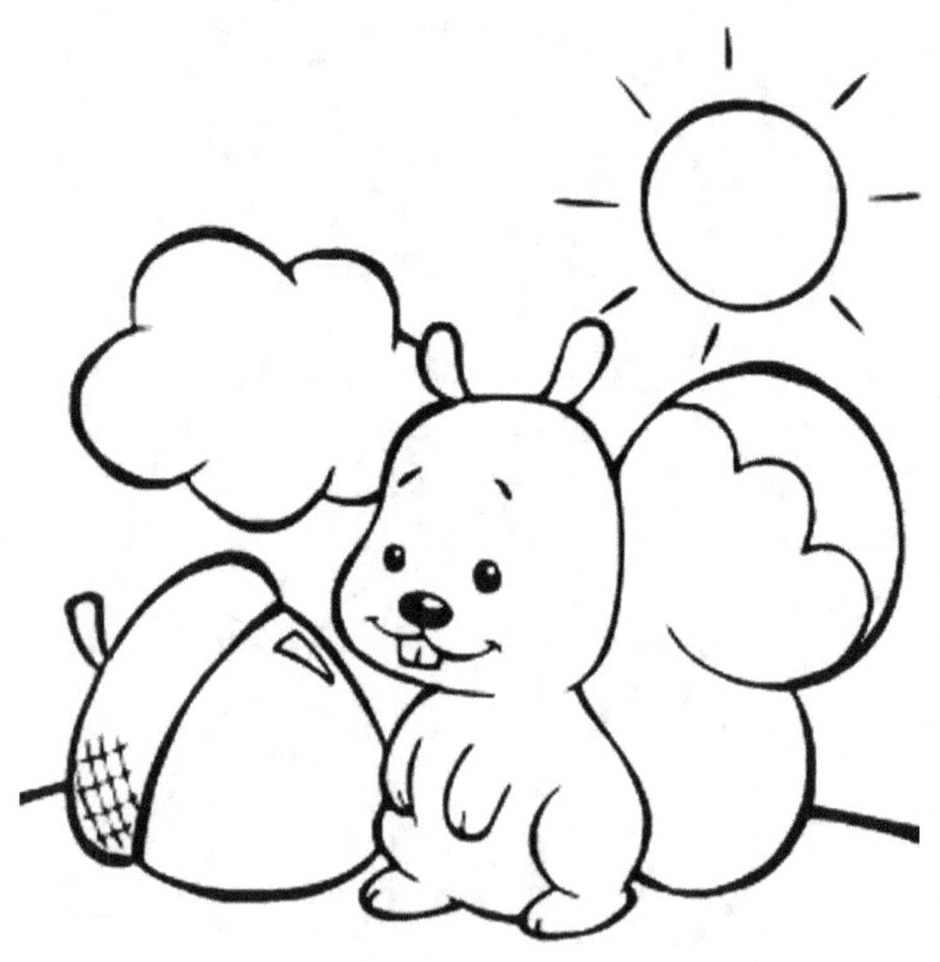

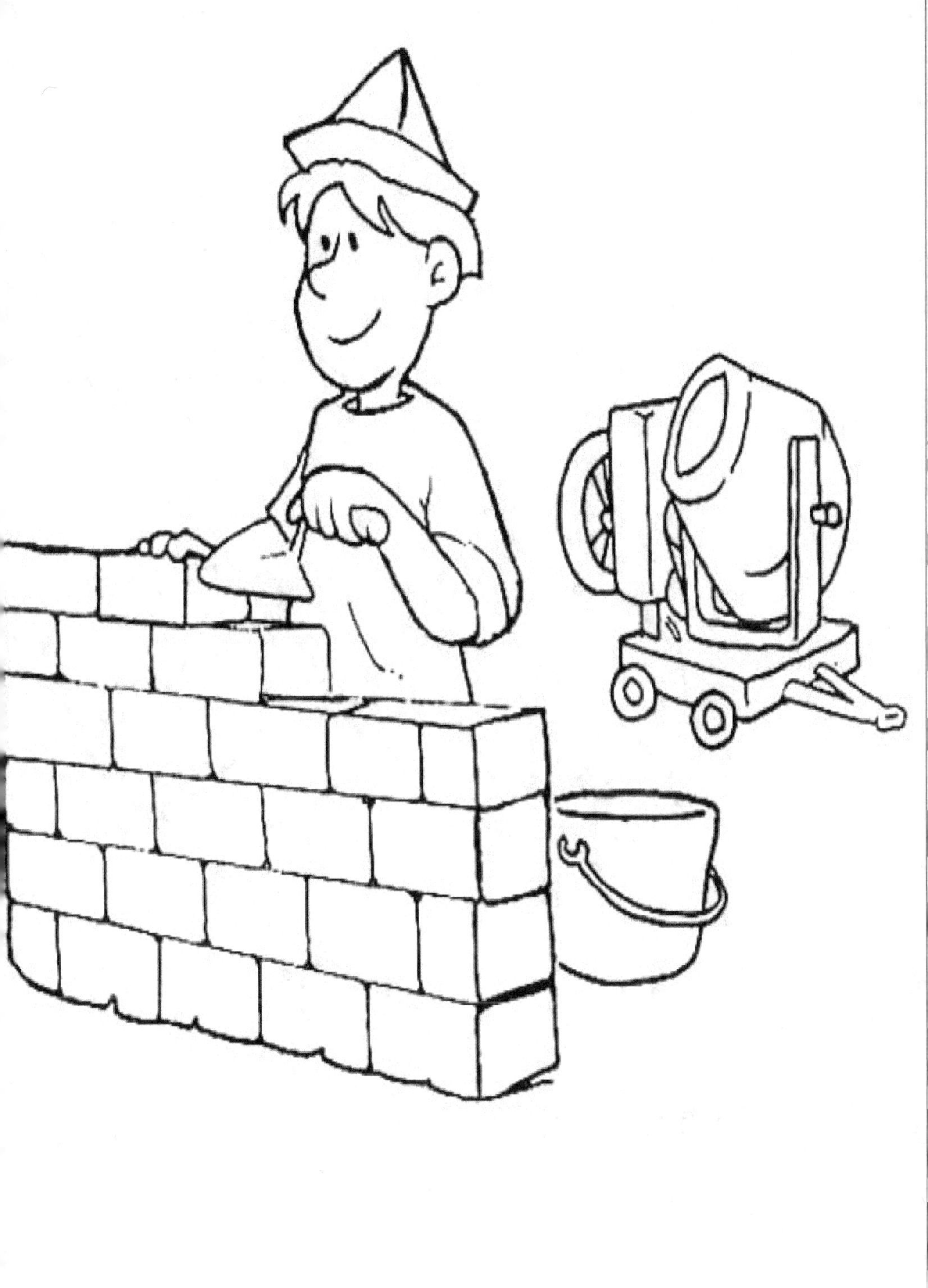

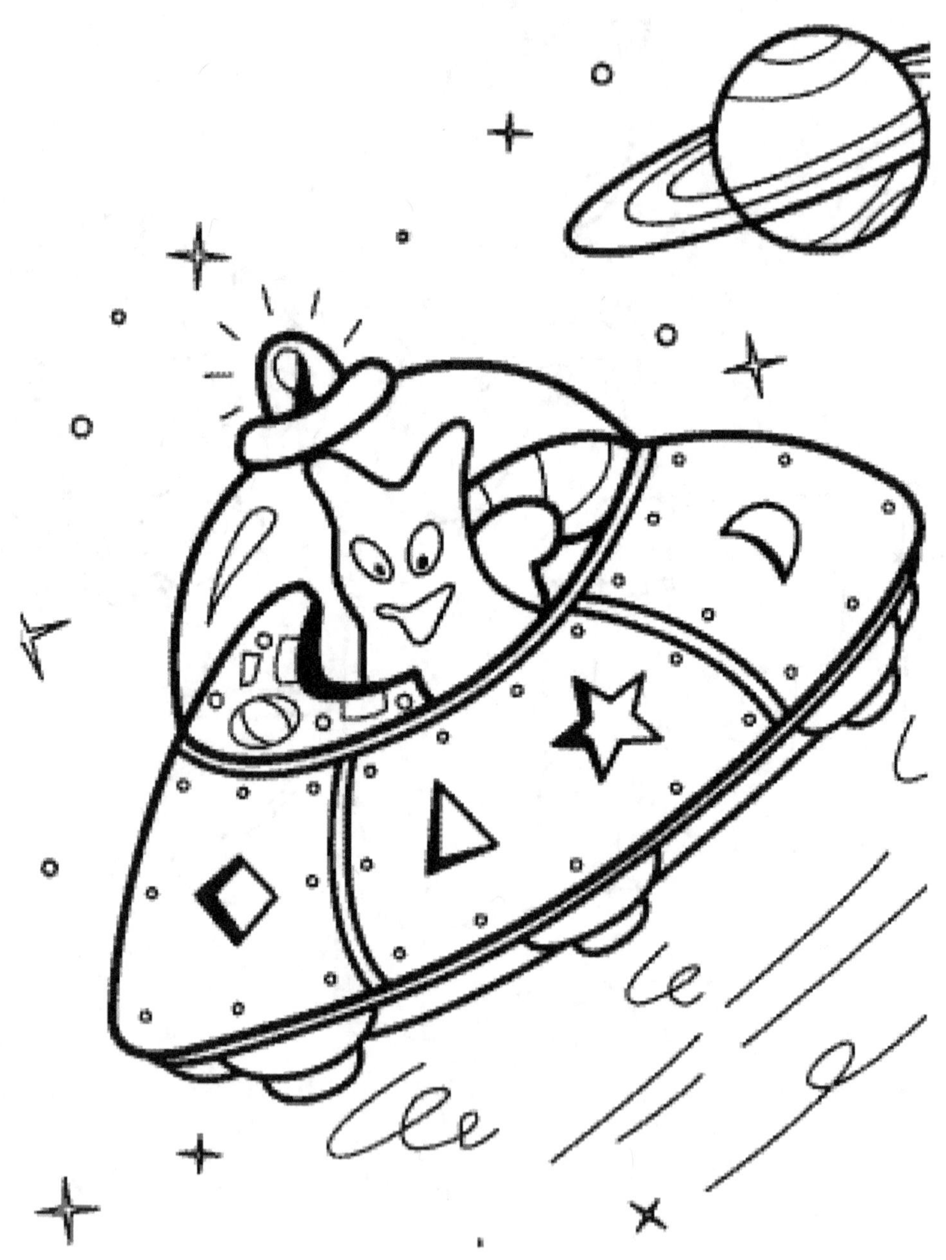

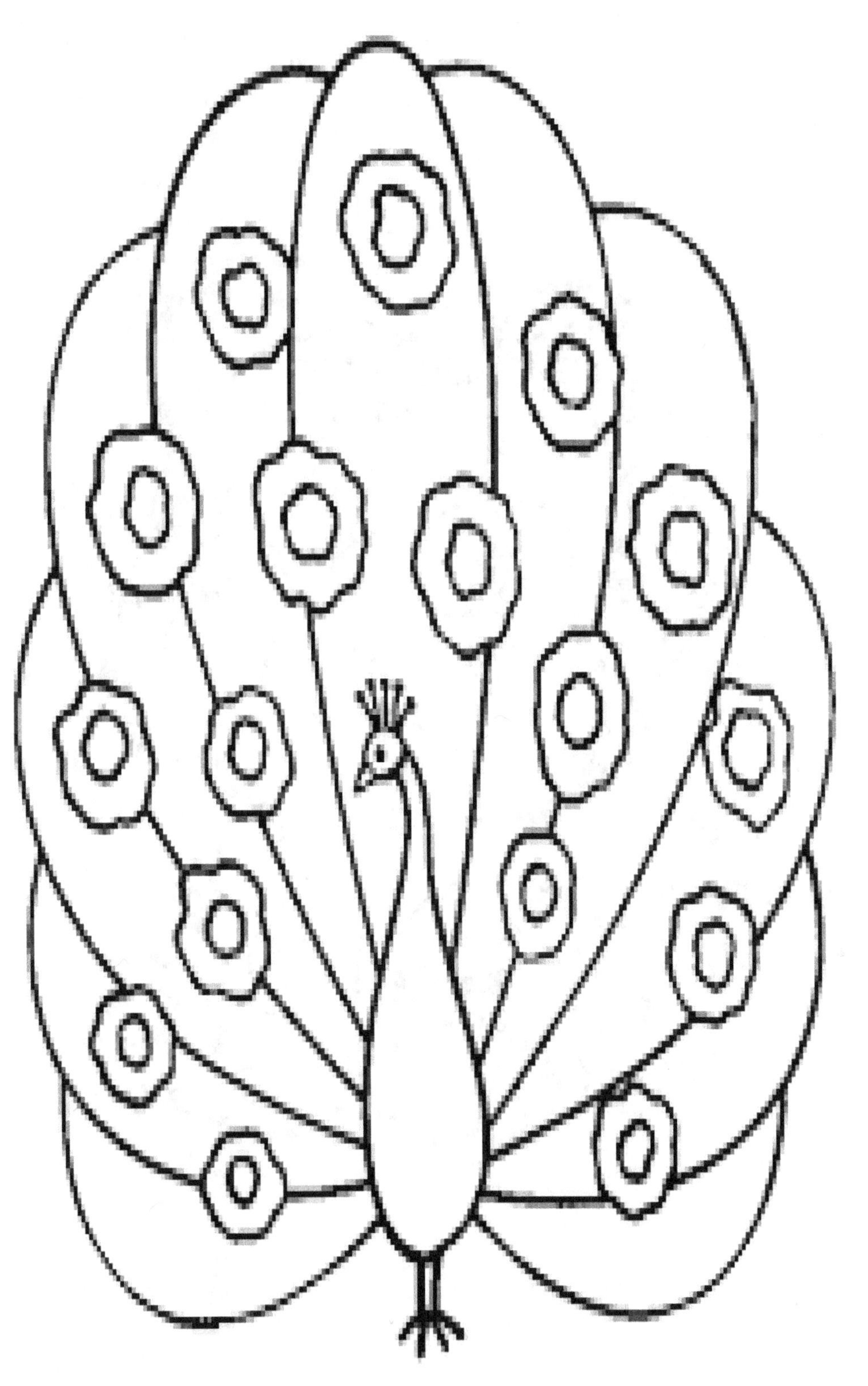

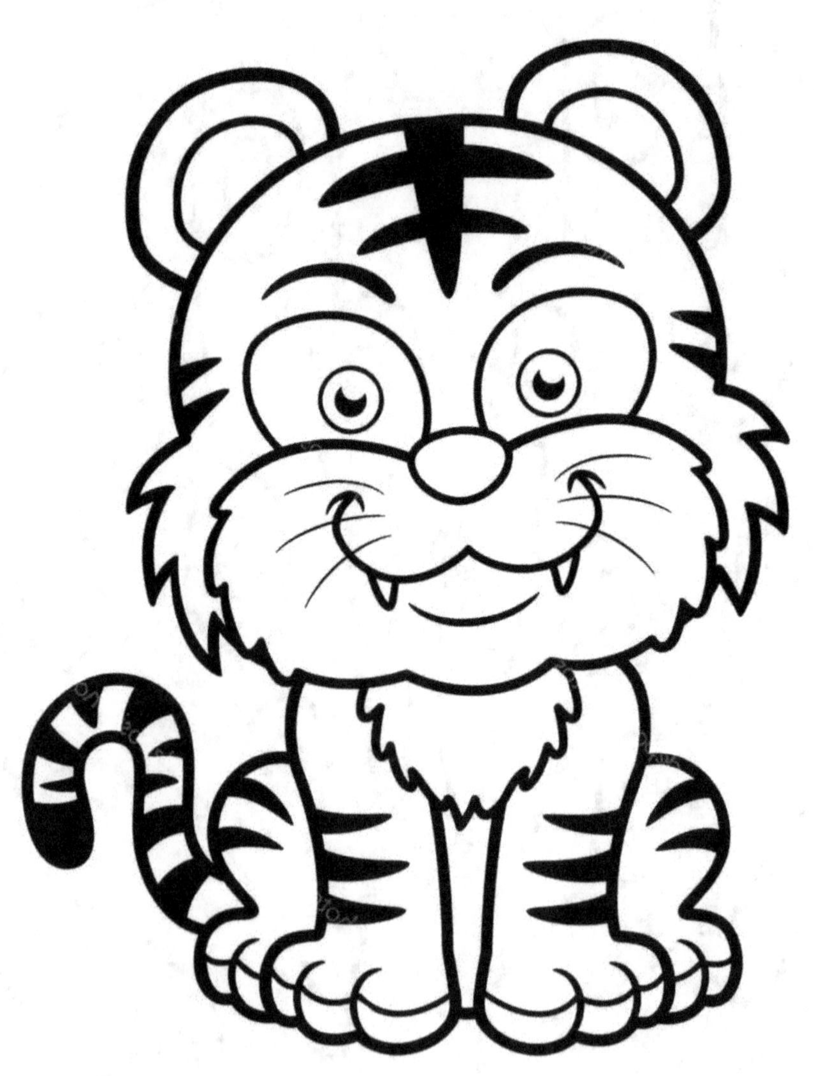

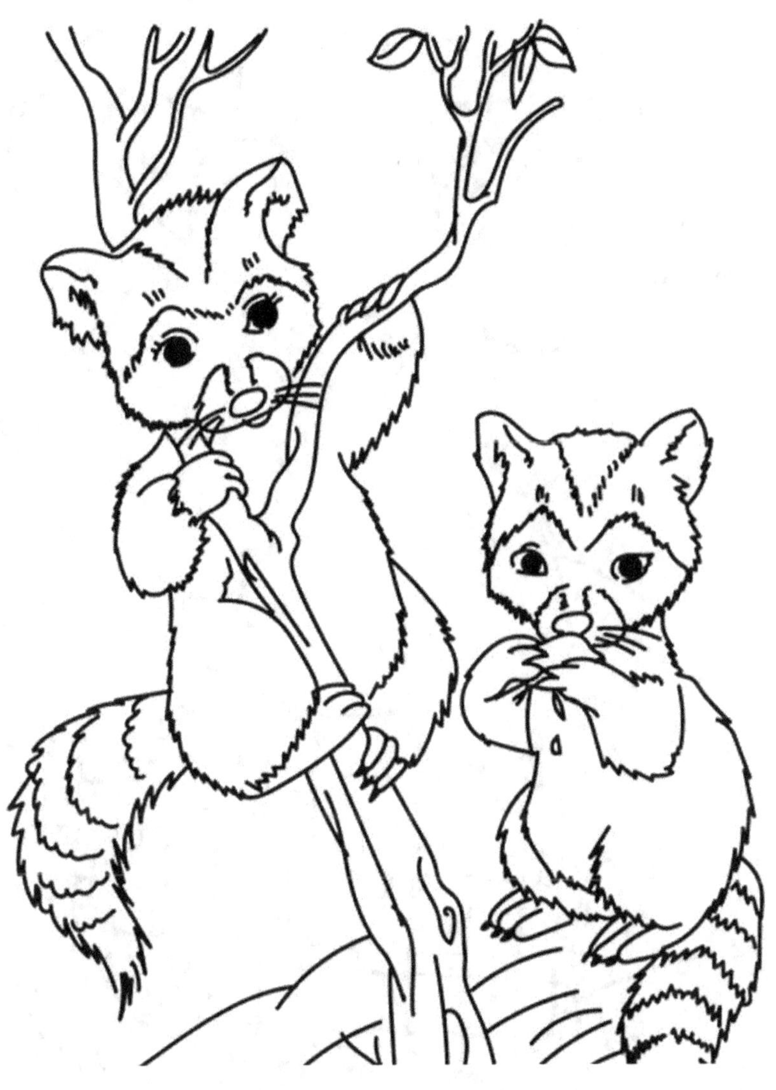

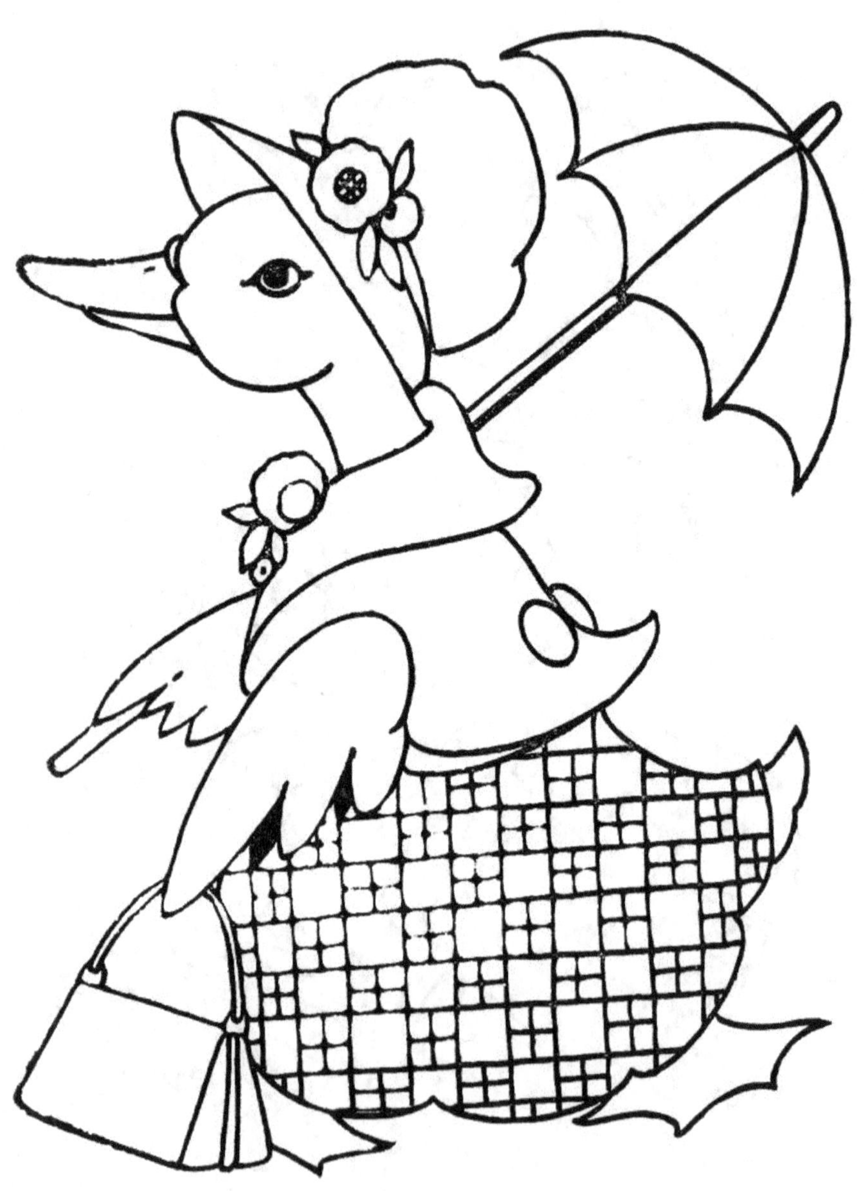

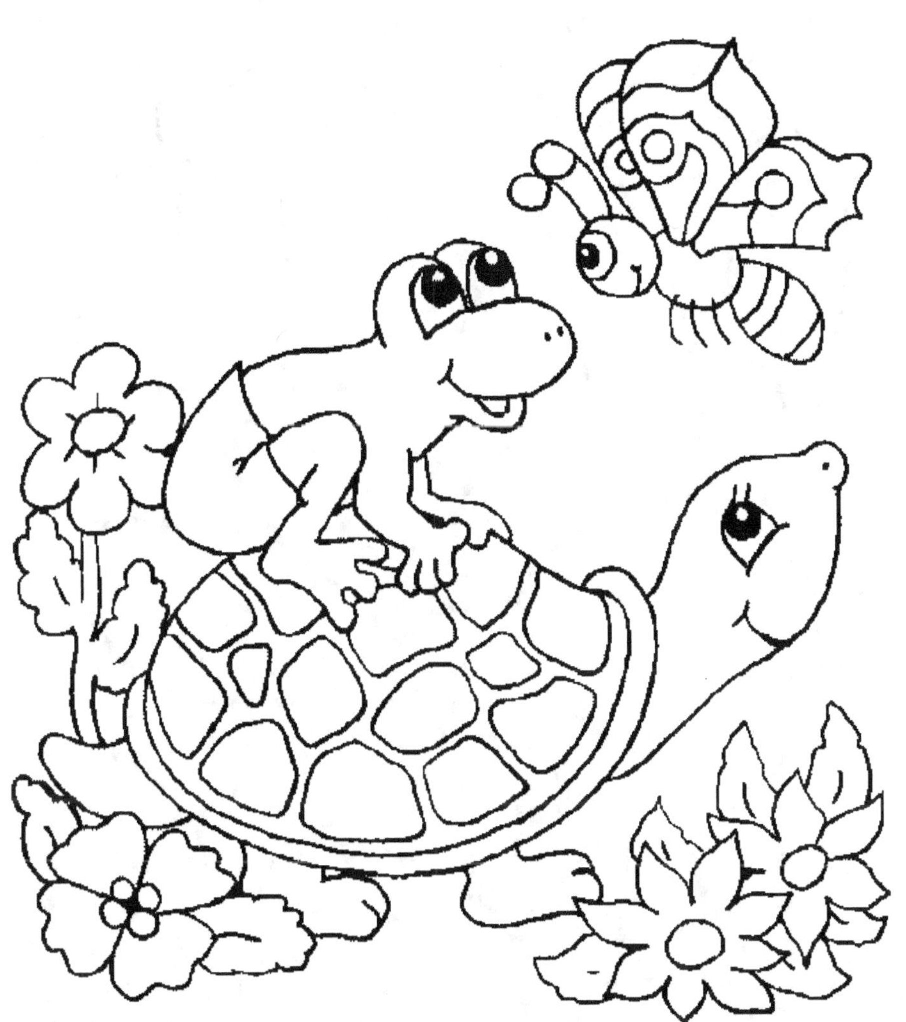

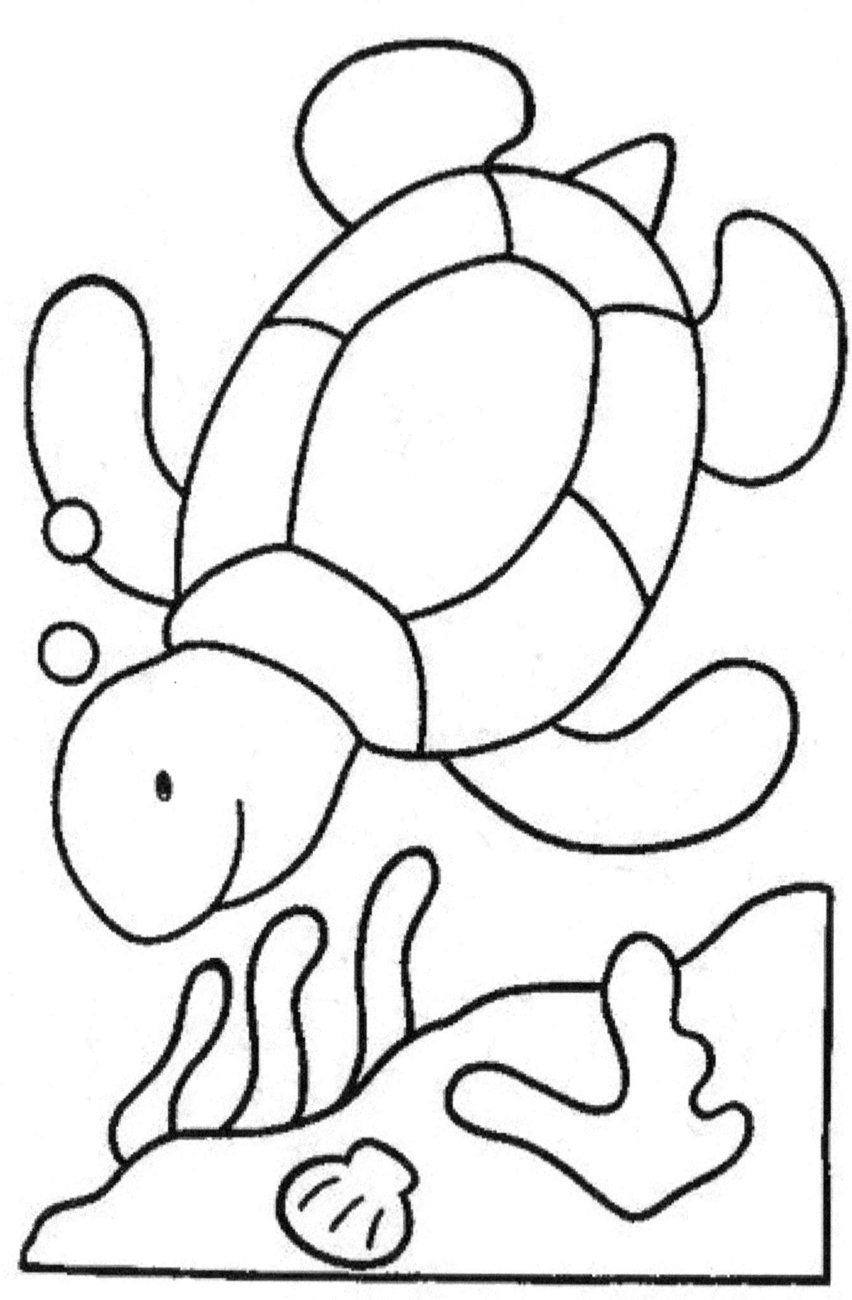

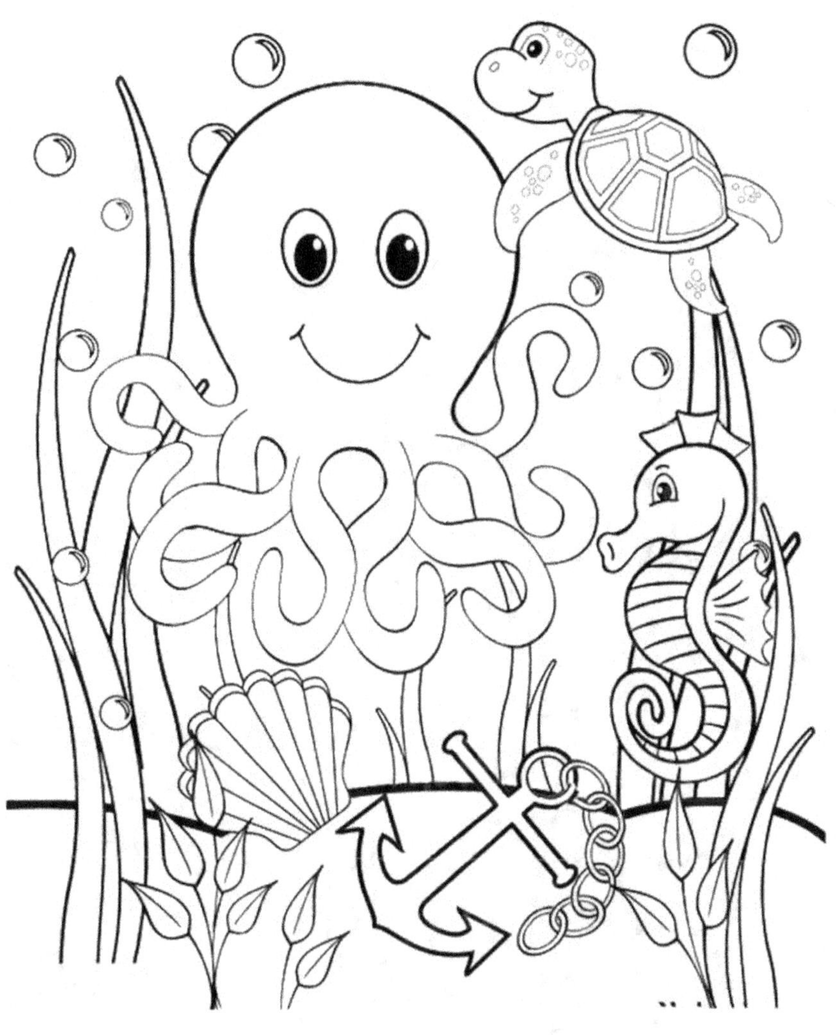

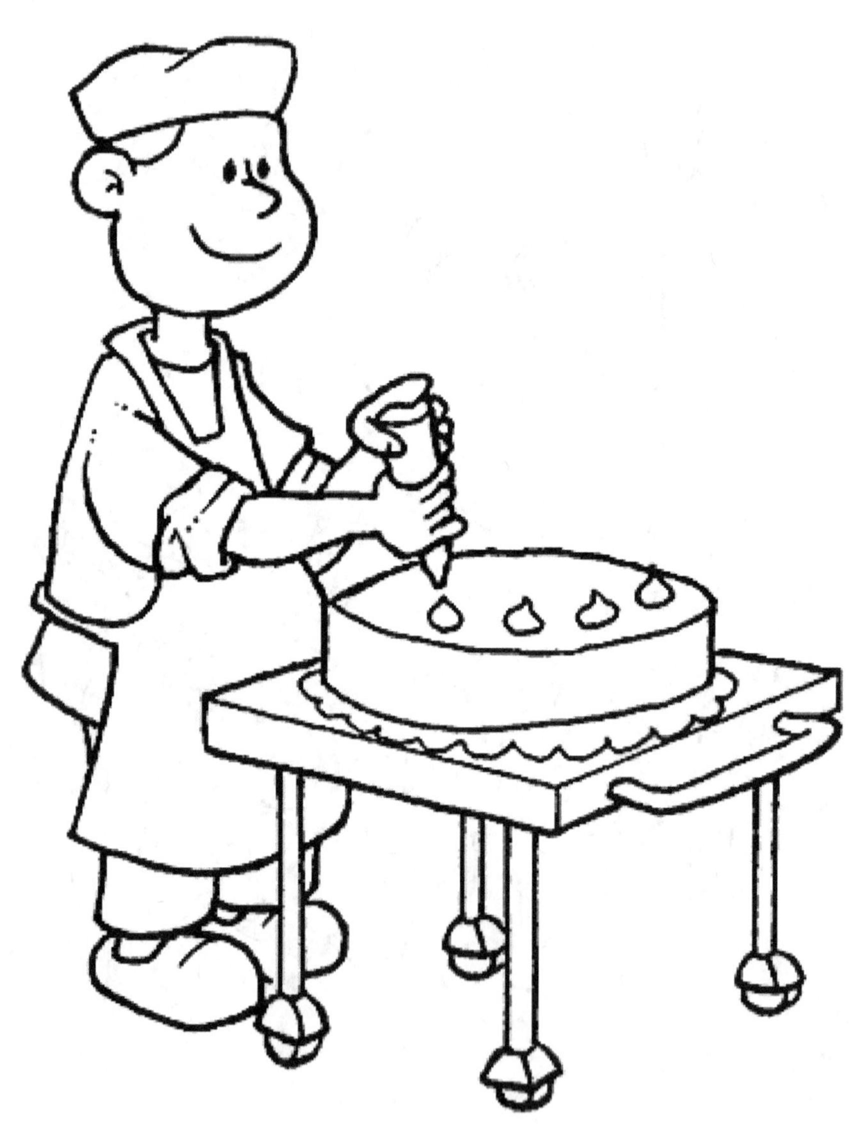

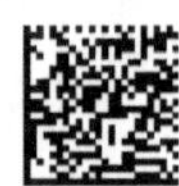

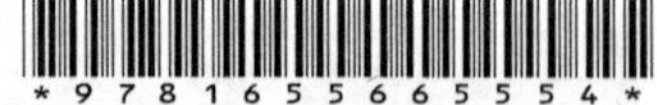